ROBIN GABY FISHER *and*
ANGELO J. GUGLIELMO, JR.

A TOUCHSTONE BOOK
PUBLISHED BY SIMON & SCHUSTER
NEW YORK   LONDON   TORONTO   SYDNEY   NEW DELHI

THE

WOMAN

The *TRUE* **STORY** *of an*
INCREDIBLE DECEPTION

WHO

WASN'T

THERE

Touchstone
A Division of Simon & Schuster, Inc.
1230 Avenue of the Americas
New York, NY 10020

First Touchstone hardcover edition April 2012

TOUCHSTONE and colophon are registered trademarks of Simon & Schuster, Inc.

For information about special discounts for bulk purchases, please contact Simon &
Schuster Special Sales at 1-866-506-1949 or business@simonandschuster.com.

The Simon & Schuster Speakers Bureau can bring authors to your live event.
For more information or to book an event, contact the Simon & Schuster
Speakers Bureau at 1-866-248-3049 or visit our website at www.simonspeakers.com.

Designed by Akasha Archer

Manufactured in the United States of America

10 9 8 7 6 5 4 3 2 1

Library of Congress Cataloging-in-Publication Data

Fisher, Robin Gaby.
  The woman who wasn't there : the true story of an incredible deception / Robin
Gaby Fisher and Angelo J. Guglielmo.
      p.   cm.
  "A Touchstone Book."
    1. Head, Tania. 2. Impostors and imposture—New York (State)—New York.
3. September 11 Terrorist Attacks, 2001 4. World Trade Center (New York, N.Y.)
I. Guglielmo, Angelo J. II. Title.
HV6760.H43F57 2012
974.7'044092—dc23
[B]
2011042089

ISBN 978-1-4516-5208-6
ISBN 978-1-4516-5210-9 (ebook)

CONTENTS

CONTENTS

CONTENTS

PROLOGUE

I used to think I was a filmmaker first, and getting the story was the only thing that mattered. And I then met Tania Head, and everything changed.

—Angelo J. Guglielmo, Jr.

THE
WOMAN
WHO
WASN'T
THERE

PART 1
2001

AUGUST 14, 2001

Tania dug her freshly painted toes into the gold-speckled sand and walked to the edge of the water where Dave was waiting. This was what she had imagined growing up. An American Prince Charming. The fairy-tale romance. A setting right out of her favorite movie. How could she be so lucky? Tania wondered. Was it possible this was all a dream? She blinked, wide awake. Dave was still there.

It was mid-August, high season in Hawaii, and a gentle breeze blew in off the Pacific, caressing Tania's bare shoulders like a warm shawl. The justice of the peace cleared his throat, a signal that the ceremony was about to begin. Just then a raucous wave crashed on shore, splashing Dave's Irish linen trousers and the skirt of Tania's white cotton beach dress. Tania and Dave looked at each other and nodded in solidarity. As the tropical sun melted on the Maui horizon, with only the local official, and two strangers from the hotel as witnesses, the beaming couple promised to love, cherish, and honor each other, through whatever came their way.

"This is the best day of my life," Tania said.

Dave nodded and pulled her close. "Me too," he said.

Sometimes Tania thought her life was too good to be true. She had lived a privileged existence. Born into a wealthy family from Barcelona, Spain, Europe's largest metropolis on the Mediterranean Sea. Growing up in the trendy l'Eixample district, the canvas for much of the early-twentieth-century masterworks of Art Nouveau architect Antoni Gaudi. Attending the best private schools money could buy. She could hardly wait to show Dave her homeland. The family residence was a short walk to the bustling Passeig de Gràcia, Spain's richest avenue, with its million-dollar apartments and fussy storefronts bearing names like Chanel and Gucci and Cartier.

Tania preferred the cobbled streets, medieval labyrinths, and rich, romantic history of the nearby Gothic Quarter, or Barri Gòtic, in the center of old Barcelona. It was in the Barri Gòtic that King Ferdinand and Queen Isabella welcomed Christopher Columbus back from his New World adventures in 1493, and Pablo Picasso abandoned traditionalism for his celebrated avant-garde style around the turn of the twentieth century. That was also where Gaudi presided over his magnum opus—construction of the Church of the Sagrada Familia—until his tragic death in 1926, when he was walking to confession and was struck by a tram. As a young girl, Tania would sit for hours in the Placa del Pi, the prettiest square in the Barri Gòtic, and watch the tourists, who came there from all over the world. The storied quarter was a fertile stage for a Catalonian schoolgirl with a prodigious imagination.

Tania had wanted for nothing growing up. Her tennis and riding skills were honed in Spain's most exclusive country clubs, and her friends hailed, as she did, from Catalonian aristocracy. Her parents spared no expense when it came to education. Tania attended prestigious Opus Dei schools—Orthodox Catholic academies with high-priced tuitions—where she studied American literature and mastered the English language at an early age.

If Tania could have changed one thing about her providential existence, it would have been to be born in America. Indeed, her infatuation with the States began when she was in grade school, and the girl begged her father to buy her an American flag, which she displayed proudly on a prominent wall in her bedroom. Her ticket to the United States had been acceptance to Harvard University, and then to the Stanford University business school, and she had planned her life precisely, quickly climbing the corporate ladder at Merrill Lynch to become its senior vice president for strategic alliances. As her career flourished, Tania lost touch with her personal life, and she had decided that maybe work was enough, when she found the man she would call her soul mate.

On the night that Dave and Tania met, in February 1999, a freezing rain was pelting downtown Manhattan. Tania, who lived in San Francisco then but often worked at Merrill Lynch's New York headquarters, had put in a fifteen-hour day at the World Trade Center, hammering out the details of a merger between a California commodities company and a rival East Coast financial firm. It was nearly midnight when she left her office in the south tower, and she was bleary eyed and eager to get back to her midtown hotel for a hot shower and the soft bed. Dave had left his office at the consulting firm of Deloitte & Touche, in the neighboring north tower, at the same hour. Taxis are scarce after dark in the financial district, and Tania sighed with relief when she spotted one idling nearby at the corner of West and Vesey Streets.

Running in her heels through puddles of slush, she was about to reach for the car door when a blustery wind caught her umbrella, turning it inside out. Ice pellets lashed her face and stung her eyes. "Great," she groaned through clenched teeth. As she wrestled the wind for the umbrella, trying not to think about her fingers, which were now numb from the cold, she almost missed the man slipping into the back of the taxi from the other side. "Hey!" she cried, yanking open her door. "You stole my cab!"

Tania often described that fateful meeting with Dave as being like a scene from a romantic comedy. There she stood, drenched and windblown, with tousled hair and a scowl on her face, and staring back at her from inside the taxi was this handsome guy, about her age, with celadon eyes and a radiant grin. As she glared at him, still trying to get her point across, he reached into his pocket and pulled out his business card. "My name is Dave," he said, seemingly amused. "You can have the cab. But you have to promise to call me." Tania grabbed the card and pushed it into the pocket of her wet wool coat. "Yeah, sure," she said, watching her runaway umbrella tumble down West Street.

Tania returned to the West Coast the following day without giving the man in the taxi another thought. But two weeks later, she was back in New York, waiting for take-out sushi in the World Trade Center concourse, when someone tapped her on the shoulder. She turned around, and there he was again. At first she couldn't place him, not until he said, "I never should have let you have that cab, because you never called."

"Oh my God," she said, flustered and groping for words.

"Can I buy you a cup of coffee?" he asked.

"Okay," she said in a faltering voice. "But I don't have much time."

Tania and Dave spent three hours talking that afternoon. She would have spent all day with him, but there was a meeting upstairs that she couldn't miss. Still, with what she had learned in that short time over coffee, Tania was smitten. Dave was twenty-four years old, two years younger than she was, and he was consulting on a long-term project for the insurance brokerage firm Marsh & McLennan. He lived uptown with two of his roommates from Penn State University, and his hope, he told Tania, was to pursue an MBA from Harvard once his project in the World Trade Center was finished. He expressed his love of the outdoors with a poem he recited for her:

You are enveloped by nature's beauty,
for just a moment you abandon your incarcerated body

What really struck Tania about Dave was not so much his good looks, or his broad range of interests and talents, or even the fact that he knew about La Diada de Sant Jordi (the annual celebration of the patron saint of Catalonia, when it is a tradition to give a rose and a book to a loved one), but that he volunteered in a soup kitchen on weekends and taught children to read for a local literacy organization. She had always considered herself a social activist.

Tania, a discreet Catalonian woman, was normally reticent about opening up to strangers, but it felt right with Dave, talking about her family and her career and her dreams for the future. She trusted him instinctively. She told him about her early life in Barcelona, about her mother being from a long line of diplomats, and that her father was a business tycoon whose work had often taken the family to the

States when she was a girl. Although she had grown up in a great class system, attending the best schools and traveling with her parents to all parts of the world, she had been taught to be humble and compassionate to those who were less fortunate. Her family didn't differentiate socially the way her status-minded counterparts did, which she considered a great gift. Social justice was in her blood, and when most of her peers were beginning to experience the tony singles bars along Las Ramblas, she was lighting candles for Miguel Angel Blanco, a member of Nuevas Generaciones, the youth arm of the People's Party of Spain, who in 1997 was kidnapped by a group of armed Basque separatists and executed when the Spanish government ignored their demand for the return of all political prisoners.

Tania shared with Dave her dreams of living in America and how, as a very young girl, she'd hung the flag on her bedroom wall. At the age of seventeen, she was recruited by Esade, then ranked by the *Wall Street Journal* as the number one international management school in the world. But when she was accepted into Harvard's early admittance program, she seized the opportunity to come to the States. The ivy-covered campus in Cambridge, Massachusetts, was everything she had imagined it would be, and she fit right in, people watching on the banks of the Charles River and listening to jazz after dark in Harvard Square. After Boston, the new age culture and Spanish influence of Northern California took her to Stanford for graduate school, and she ended up settling in San Francisco.

"I have to see you again," Dave told Tania when they parted that day.

"As long as you don't steal another cab," she said, trying to sound coy.

After several months of exorbitant phone bills and bicoastal dating, they fell in love. Tania eventually moved to New York, and they bought an enormous apartment together in an exclusive building on the Upper East Side and a golden retriever puppy they named Elvis. Money was no object. They bought whatever they wanted and flew off for weekends on a whim. She was a rising star at Merrill Lynch, and he postponed his plans to attend Harvard when his consulting company promoted him to a senior management position. They had achieved the American Dream, and they weren't even thirty years old. Although their meeting seemed coincidental, they both believed it was destiny. A wedding day was inevitable.

Tania loved recalling the day in the early spring of 2001, when they had been together for over a year, and Dave surprised her with the marriage proposal during dinner at Windows on the World. They chose October 12 as their wedding date: the National Day of Spain. The wedding would be planned to Tania's mother's specifications at the Plaza Hotel on Fifth Avenue and Central Park South, in the gilded Terrace Room, with five hundred guests and all the trimmings of a high society affair.

A few months wasn't much time to plan such a spectacular social splash, however, and the pressure of the task mounted with all of the decisions that had to be made. Tania and Dave, who both were exacting and obstinate, began bickering over every detail, right down to the filling in the wedding cake and the color of his morning coat. It didn't help that Dave's mother was always fussing about this or that. You would have thought that it was *her* wedding, Tania complained to a friend.

By summer, Tania and Dave were fighting every day. Dave's mother was making so many demands that the tension had reached a breaking point, and Tania wasn't even sure she wanted to go through with the wedding. But her doubts dissolved when, on one particularly steamy August night, she was reminded why she had fallen for Dave in the first place. Tania had dragged herself home from work and pushed open the apartment door to find a path of rose petals inside. She followed the petal trail down the hall and into the dining room, where she found Dave, dressed in a coconut bra and a grass skirt, dancing the hula to a recording by Don Ho. On the dining room table were steaming dishes of Hawaiian food that Dave had prepared from recipes he'd found on the Internet, and two plane tickets to Hawaii for the next day.

Tania had been to Hawaii, but never to the Grand Wailea Resort on the beach in Maui, and it was spectacular. Dave had booked a sprawling suite with panoramic views of the orchid trees and the ocean that was usually reserved for celebrities. Barbra Streisand, George Clooney, and Julia Roberts were just a few of the A-listers who had stayed there, he told Tania. She was enchanted by the place.

It was their third day on the island when Dave announced that he had a surprise.

"What? Another one?" Tania asked.

"It's just beginning," he said.

Dave had scheduled an afternoon in the hotel's famous Spa Grande. After a couple's massage, Tania was given the royal treatment. Dave had arranged for her to have a manicure and pedicure. A stylist combed her hair into a loose upsweep, and a makeup artist applied pink stain to her lips and cheeks. When she was all finished, a hotel employee appeared at the door to her changing room with a white garment bag.

"What is this?" Tania asked.

"Please, put it on," the woman replied.

Inside the bag was a simple but beautiful long white dress hanging from a satin-covered hanger. Tania slipped into it, and the garment fit as if it were made just for her.

"Shoes?" Tania asked.

"No, no," the woman said. "Just your bare feet."

The woman motioned for Tania to follow her out of the spa. As they walked through the hotel's ornate lobby, four brawny men dressed as ancient Hawaiian tribal warriors, carrying fiery torches, met them. They escorted Tania from the hotel to the beach, where Dave was standing by the water, in the middle of a circle of white orchids.

"Will you marry me?" he asked. "Right here? Right now?"

The ceremony had been magical, and, after a dinner under the stars, Tania and Dave called their families and friends to announce that they were "Mauied." Their parents could only be mollified by assurances from the newlyweds that the "official" wedding at the Plaza would still take place on October 12 as planned.

Standing under the stars, Tania found herself worrying about the price of such unadulterated joy. Happiness was fleeting, so how long could they possibly expect their lives to remain one long continuum of bliss?

Watching waves lap the shoreline, she felt Dave's hand brush her face.

"Where are you?" he asked.

"I was just thinking that I never want this to end," she said.

"It never will," he said, deep dimples pleating his chiseled face.

SEPTEMBER 11

At 8:46 a.m., one hour and six minutes after pushing back from the gate at Boston Logan International Airport, American Airlines Flight 11, a Boeing 767 carrying eighty-one passengers and ten thousand gallons of fuel, and moving 470 miles an hour, plowed through the upper floors of the World Trade Center's north tower. At the time, Tania was conducting a meeting in Merrill Lynch's conference room on the ninety-sixth floor of the south tower. The meeting had just convened, and members of her team were grumbling about the end of summer and the finality of a merger they'd been working on for months, which meant that, regrettably, they would soon be going their separate ways. All at once, the building shook, and the lights in the conference room flickered. People outside the closed door squealed.

"What the hell happened?" one of Tania's colleagues asked.

"I'll go check it out," another team member said.

"No, no," Tania insisted. "Let me go."

People in the office were gaping out the windows facing the neighboring skyscraper.

"What is it?" Tania asked.

"The north tower is on fire," a woman said plaintively.

The phones on the floor were ringing off the hook, but people couldn't seem to tear themselves away from the windows to answer. Tania joined the others and couldn't believe what she was seeing. Giant balls of fire shot from a gaping hole toward the top of the breached building, and plumes of black smoke coiled around the top floors like a giant snake. People speculated about what could have caused the wreckage. Had it been another bomb, like the one detonated in the basement of the north tower eight years earlier? Maybe a small plane, or a helicopter, or a commuter flight? They were always flying too close to the towers.

Standing there, Tania tried calling Dave but got that pulsing "circuit's busy" sound. So she pressed her face to the glass and counted down stories from the top of the adjacent skyscraper to the ninety-eighth floor offices of Marsh & McLennan. An accumulating sense of dread swept over her as she counted down. "One hundred one, one hundred, ninety-nine . . ." Dave's floor was burning and belching smoke. The fireball was so intense that she could feel the heat radiating from the other tower. As she stared at the gloomy scene across the way, disbelieving, powerless, wondering what to do, a chorus of horrified screams broke out among her coworkers.

Tania didn't grasp what was happening, not at first. Not until a colleague cried out that someone was about to jump from the north tower. She looked toward the top of the burning skyscraper and saw a man teetering on a ledge outside the Windows on the World restaurant. It had only been a few months earlier that she and Dave were there on the one hundred seventh floor, having that romantic dinner, and he dropped to one knee and proposed. "How could life have gone from that to this?" Tania wondered, watching the horrified reaction of her colleagues to the desperate man, clinging to the building, a quarter mile in the sky. One thing was certain: whatever was happening in the other tower was going to change all of their lives.

As the number of wary spectators grew, everyone jostling for a look at the unfolding disaster, Tania struggled to keep her place at the window. She recalled reading once that the architect of the World Trade Center, Minoru Yamasaki, had a fear of heights and purposely designed the towers with small windows to make them feel more secure. On her first day on the job on the ninety-sixth floor, she had nevertheless suffered from a dreadful bout of vertigo and worried that she wouldn't be able to work in the building. The sensation had only lasted a day, though, and she didn't experience it again. Not until she saw the man on the ledge, and then she felt as if the floor beneath her were falling away.

In a few short minutes, the black smoke swirling around the top of the north tower had gotten so dense that Tania could no longer see the man. But others had begun dropping from the upper floors, spiraling inelegantly against a void blue sky toward a certain and terrible death. One after the other, men and women plunged out of gaping holes and broken windows, thrashing and flailing, trying against impossible odds to hold on to what was left of their lives. At first Tania thought they were blown out of the building. But, watching closely, she could see some of them making conscious choices to die by falling rather than by fire. Defiant in the face of death, they would at least choose how to end their lives. Could one of them be Dave? One man leapt and immediately began flapping his arms, as if he were trying to fly. It was that moment, watching the poor man's macabre attempt to save himself, that Tania decided to leave the south tower, despite the voice on the public address system insisting that their building was safe. "We have to get out of here," Tania said to her coworkers. "Now!"

The World Trade Center elevator system required people to take two elevators between the ground and the upper floors. Passengers rode nonstop express elevators to transfer lobbies on the forty-fourth and seventy-eighth floors, where they walked across a hallway to catch smaller elevators to the higher stories. Rather than wait for the local elevator to shuttle them down from the ninety-sixth to the seventy-eighth floor, Tania decided to walk down the eighteen flights to the sky lobby and catch an express to the ground from there. "This way!" she called over her shoulder. Only her assistant Christine had followed her to the stairs.

The seventy-eighth-floor sky lobby was jammed with people poised between going up or down. Did they listen to their instincts and leave the building? Or heed the advice of the security officers who encouraged them to return to their offices rather than put themselves in harm's way outside in the plaza? Tania pushed her way from the emergency stairwell into the crush of bodies, pulling Christine in behind her. The lines for the express elevators, each capable of descending to the ground in a minute, stretched from one end of the lobby to the other. Everyone was jittery, nudging and elbowing one another, trying to get closer to the front. It smelled like fear.

Christine was trembling and near tears. There was no reason to be afraid, Tania said, trying to console her. The voice on the public address system said the south tower was safe. But even as she tried to reassure her assistant, Tania had a gnawing feeling in her stomach. What had happened in the other building? Rumors were flying, but no one knew for sure. People carrying BlackBerry phones were able to get sporadic messages from the outside and shared whatever news they had, but it wasn't much.

If only she knew that Dave was all right. Tania looked at her phone. No service. "Damn," she said. The phone slipped through her clammy hands. With people standing shoulder to shoulder, there was barely room to bend down to pick it up. No one was willing to move for fear of losing his or her place in line. Was it her imagination, Tania wondered, or were the elevators taking forever?

As cars arrived and left, some packed so tightly that the last people in were pushed out, Tania tried to stay calm. Her mind was made up. She was leaving, and panicking wouldn't get her any closer to getting out of the building and finding Dave. The first thing that she was going to do when she finally saw him was to apologize for the dustup over his mother's birthday present that morning.

On the subway on the way to work, Dave had said he wanted to buy some silly tchotchke for his mom. Tania thought that they should get something nice or, at the very least, treat her to a birthday dinner at the restaurant of her choice. They were still arguing when she left him at the turnstile in the World Trade Center Plaza at seven thirty, and he headed up to his office. She had taken a few extra minutes to finish her coffee and bran muffin before going up to work a little before eight. Thirty minutes later, Dave called her, wanting to make up. He didn't like it when they argued. "Want to grab a quick cup of coffee downstairs?" he asked. "Can't," she had said dismissively. "I'm just about to go into a meeting." Had she even said good-bye?

Elevators came and went, but the lines in the sky lobby didn't seem to move. Tania took a deep breath through her nostrils and then exhaled slowly. It was a relaxation technique called *pranayama* that she had learned in her yoga class. "Focus on the breath," the instructor had said. "Pay attention to the flow of air as it moves in and out of your body." Purposefully, mindfully, she inhaled deeply into the pit of her stomach, up through her chest to her collarbones, and then slowly released the breath through her nose. After a few breaths, her heart seemed to settle down a bit. Tania wasn't necessarily a religious woman, but now she prayed that Dave had gone down for coffee without her. Of course he had. Soon it would be her turn on the elevator, and she would find him down on the street, waiting for her. The time was right around nine o'clock.

At that moment, United Airlines Flight 175 was screaming across New York Harbor. The Boeing 767, also bound from Boston to Los Angeles, carried fifty-six passengers, two pilots, and seven flight attendants. It passed the Statue of Liberty, banked hard left, and hurtled toward the south tower. Tania heard what sounded like the whine of a hundred airplanes. A woman standing near a window at the south end of the sky lobby screamed.

"Another plane is coming! Another plane is coming!"

At first Tania thought that the woman was just hysterical. But the sound of jet engines grew louder and more ominous. "What's going on?" Christine cried. Tania grabbed her assistant and embraced her. "I'll take care of you," she said.

Everything happened so quickly after that. The sickening scream of the jet engines as the plane advanced with impossible speed. People crying. People screaming. People dropping to their knees in prayer. There would be no escape, no safe berth, Tania thought, as the roar grew louder and meaner. "It's coming for us," she said to herself. "We're all going to die right here." The windows exploded in a million shards of glass. Tania saw the silver wing of the United jet slice through the sky lobby, shredding everything in its path. The force of the impact tore Christine from her arms. Marble walls disintegrated, and whole sections of ceiling collapsed. The building bowed sideways, and then snapped back fiercely. An elevator filled with people disappeared down a black, bottomless shaft. Tania was caught in a ferocious wave of heat. She felt as if her lungs were on fire and she couldn't take a breath. She realized that she was flying through the air, toward the bank of elevators, where flames were shooting from the empty shafts. "Please let this be over fast," she prayed. "I know I'm going to die. Please don't make it hurt."

She awakened under a jagged slab of marble, to the stench of burning flesh. Gagging, she suddenly realized that she was smelling her own skin burning. The sky lobby, which moments before had been bustling with people, was a snarl of twisted steel, pulverized wallboard, and dangling wires. The elevator shafts glowed red, and in the dim light of the small fires seething around her, Tania could make out the bodies. The lobby was strewn with the dead and the dying. A vast canvas of grief. Rolling over to try to free herself, she realized that she was lying beside a mortally injured person. She recognized the dress on the headless torso. It was Christine.

Tania let out a long, silent scream. "These are the very last moments of my life," she thought. "Why does it have to end now? Why does it have to end here, like this?"

It was getting harder to breathe. Blinded by dense smoke, she didn't know where she was, and she didn't know how to get out. Looking over the carnage, she recognized the remains of some of her other coworkers. They must have followed her down the stairs after all. She had led all of them to a merciless death. Her anxiety turned to despair and finally to resignation: She would never get to wear the white princess gown she had chosen for her upcoming wedding. She would never get to tell Dave she was sorry for bickering with him that morning. "It's no use," she thought, surrendering to the sound of her own death knell. She would die in the south tower too.

Then, just as Tania closed her eyes, she felt someone slapping her back, causing her a nauseous kind of pain. She swung with her good arm. "Why are you hurting me?" she cried, by then nearly delirious. "Please stop hurting me." Kneeling over her was a man with a red bandanna wrapped around his face. He wasn't trying to hurt her. He was patting down her burning clothes with his jacket. The man's eyes were kind and knowing.

"Are you real?" Tania asked.

"Just stay awake," he said. "Stay awake."

Tania clung to the sound of his voice. "I found a stairway," he said. "I'm going to show you the way. Can you get up? Are you able to make it to the stairs?"

Tania wiggled her toes and then moved her legs. "I think I can," she said. Pain coursed through her body as she slowly rose to her feet. Her right arm dangled from a thread of sinew, and she tucked it into her jacket pocket to keep it from falling off. With the man in the red bandanna supporting her, she walked over bodies and body parts.

"I don't think I can go on," she said, wiping blood from her forehead.

"Just keep moving," he said, his voice strong and unwavering.

Trudging forward, her attention was drawn to a sudden, slight movement in the sea of stillness. She could barely make out the form of a man in the murkiness, a man camouflaged by a knot of grisly bodies and his own terrible burns. "Wait," Tania said, kneeling beside him. Gasping for breath, the dying man reached for her. "Please give this to my wife," he said, dropping something hot into her hand. The gold wedding band in her palm was inscribed with a woman's name and the word *Forever*. Tania wiped away tears as she stared into the man's eyes. "I'll find her and I'll give it to her," she promised, placing the ring in her pocket, but the man was already gone.

"The stairway is just ahead," the man with the red bandanna said, summoning Tania forward. "We're almost there. You can't help him now."

The door to the stairs was partially blocked by debris, but there was enough room to squeeze through. The stairwell was stuffy, and smatterings of ghoulish-looking people were slowly making their way down. Panic-stricken, Tania turned to her rescuer. "I'm so scared!" she cried. "Go," he said, putting his hand on her shoulder. "You can do this." Tania trusted the stranger. It wasn't like her to give up, and she had so much to live for. She thought of the beautiful white princess wedding gown hanging in her closet at home. She had spent weeks searching for just the right dress for the formal ceremony, and it was perfect. The wedding was only a month away. Dave would be sick with worry by now. Taking a deep breath, she pressed through the doorway and began her descent.

When she turned to look back, the man with the red bandanna was walking back into the smoke.

A LONG WAY DOWN

Will you stay with me, will you be my love
Among the fields of barley

Tania sang in a low whisper. She was certain that she would lose her mind if she stopped. As it was, her sanity was cracking. Singing her favorite Sting songs helped to muffle the ominous echoes of crashing planes and doomed coworkers that were trapped inside her head. Others in the stairwell moved forward slowly, single file, looking dazed, saying nothing. The stairs were slick with a paste of water spilling from broken pipes and powder from pulverized Sheetrock. Tania was puzzled by how orderly things seemed in the narrow passageway. They were traumatized people navigating a long, uncertain procession from hell, yet no one panicked or pushed to get ahead.

Occasionally someone glanced at her and then quickly looked away. She must have been a sight, she thought, burned and bleeding, covered in a fine, gray dust, her tattered jacket hanging in shreds from her blackened torso. But her mangled right arm was the worst. It was still tucked into her jacket pocket, but she didn't know how long it would stay attached. Tania was light-headed and beyond weary, with no way of knowing what was ahead of her. She had hobbled down probably only two or three stories since leaving the man with the red bandanna on the seventy-eighth floor, but it felt like fifty. Each flight seemed longer and harder than the last, and she didn't want to think about how many more there were to go until she would finally reach the bottom. With each movement, an ungodly pain tore through her body, and she tried not to scream. So with every agonizing step, she sang.

Oh can't you see
you belong to me
Now my poor heart aches
with every step you take

There was a moment when she didn't know where she was anymore. It felt as if she were drifting outside of her body. She thought, "I'm already dead!" and maybe all of the people around her were dead, too, ghostly troops marching toward some godforsaken afterlife. But then her stoic Catalan resolve kicked in and, like a thunderclap in the dead of night, snapped Tania out of her delirium. No, she wasn't dead, and she wasn't going to die. Not like this. Not in some grim, gray stairwell.

Soldiering on, she thought about her family back in Spain and her upcoming wedding at the Plaza. And Dave. Her beloved Dave. What would he say if he knew she hadn't tried her best to survive? What floor was she on, anyway? She didn't even know. The heat in the stairway was suffocating, and with every step forward, her breath became more labored. Tania's eyes stung, and her lungs felt as if they were burning from the inside out. Her vision blurred, and, when she winced, silvery stars darted behind her closed eyelids. The stairwell started to spin, faster and faster it went, and, all at once, she was six years old and playing with her classmates at the Opus Dei School in Barcelona. They were skipping in a circle and singing, "Here we go round the mulberry bush, the mulberry bush, the mulberry bush. Here we go round the mulberry bush. On a cold and frosty morning." The sweet sound of her own childlike voice soothed her. Then everything went dark.

When Tania came to, she was lying alone on the hard stairs. She tried moving, but her legs were lame. Was it her brain or her body getting in the way? she wondered. Somehow she had to get herself out of the building. She heard her father's voice. "In this family, we don't give up, we overcome," he always said. Just then a clatter of voices wafted up from somewhere below her, and she spotted a small pack of firefighters, loaded down with heavy equipment, trudging up the steps. She held out her hand.

"I've got this one," one of them said, stooping beside her limp body and signaling the others to go ahead.

The young New York City firefighter was breathless and dripping sweat. Kneeling over her, he spoke reassuringly. His eyes were soft and kind, but she saw him look at her dangling arm.

"Okay, sweetheart," he said. "You're going to be okay. I'm going to get you out of here. Can you put your good arm around me?"

Tania fought to stay awake. People upstairs were dying, and they needed to be saved. "The seventy-eighth floor," she said in a weak, shaky voice. "There are people up there who are terribly hurt."

"Help is on the way for them," the firefighter said. "Now, let's get you out of here."

Tania rose slowly to her knees and, with the firefighter's help, forced herself to her feet. She was weak and wobbly, and her heart pounded out of her chest. Leaning heavily on his arm, she walked down one step, then another, and another. She could feel the building shaking and swaying. She tried to sing, but the words no longer came.

"You're doing great," the firefighter said, encouraging her, willing her to go on. "We're getting there. You can do it. Only twenty flights to go."

She stumbled going from one step to the next and then stopped. Twenty flights? They still had to walk down twenty flights?

"I can't go any farther!" she cried. "I'm sorry, but I can't make it. I can't make it!"

"We're leaving here together," he said, his voice strong and commanding. "I'm going to carry you the rest of the way."

The brawny young firefighter lifted her up, and the coarseness of his jacket against her cheek was somehow comforting. Tania had always prided herself on being fiercely independent: making her own money, putting herself through Harvard, then Stanford, climbing to the top of the financial industry, which was still a man's world. But she needed this man now. She needed him if she was going to get out of that building and survive, if she was ever going to see Dave again, and she didn't even know the firefighter's name. They descended the stairs slowly, strangers bonded by the fragile line between life and death—he, talking about fishing with his kids; she, saying nothing for fear that words would steal the last vestiges of air in her lungs.

At last they reached the lobby. What had been a bright, welcoming expanse of open space was now a gray, murky cavern. Windows were broken and chandeliers smashed. Burst pipes gushed water over cracked marble walls, and empty black cavities stood where elevators had once been. The firefighter pushed through the wreckage and ran for the warped revolving doors leading outside to the World Trade Center Plaza. As he carried her through a shattered panel of glass to the outside, she heard a succession of rattling explosions. People were running and screaming. She arched her head slightly to see bodies and body parts strewn over the plaza. The explosions were the bodies of jumpers hitting the pavement. Before she had time to react, the firefighter was passing her to one of his colleagues. "Get her to an ambulance!" he barked, turning and rushing back toward the tower.

It was only a moment or so later when a terrible sound, like steel bending and groaning, aching for release, thundered overhead. Tania heard loud snapping and cracking sounds. The second firefighter, with Tania in his arms, sprinted toward a parked ladder engine and dove beneath it, throwing his body over hers. A low rumble got louder and louder, until it sounded as if a freight train were speeding through the plaza. People were screaming that the tower was falling, and "Run! Run!" Then a titanic crash.

A torrent of debris rained down, covering the fire truck. She felt the firefighter put his oxygen mask over her face. They were in total darkness. Buried alive.

* * *

When Tania opened her eyes again, she was lying under a blinding white light, surrounded by people with furrowed brows and green surgical masks.

"Where am I?" she asked, bewildered, and trying to focus on the worried faces looking down at her.

"I'm a doctor," one of them said. "You're in New York—Presbyterian Hospital. Can you tell me your name?"

"Tania," she replied, her throat parched and scratchy.

"Can you tell us your last name, Tania?"

"My name is Tania Head," she said, struggling to speak because of the tube in her mouth and running down her throat.

"Do you know why you're here?" the doctor asked.

Tania's brain felt fuzzy. She shook her head, trying to expel the blurriness, and, just as she did, an arrow of burning pain pierced her right shoulder. Instinctively, she felt for her arm. It was still there. Then she tugged at the tube in her mouth, but a nurse gently guided her hand away, explaining that the tube was helping her to breathe.

"Tania," the doctor said, prodding gently, "do you remember what happened to you?"

She didn't want to remember, didn't want to answer the doctor's question about whether she knew why she was lying in a hospital, panicked and afraid, with oxygen streaming into her lungs and most of her upper body wrapped in white gauze. Closing her eyes, she wished that she could forget about everything she had seen and felt as she fought her way out of that ravaged death trap, climbing over smoldering bodies and people who were dying, to save her own life.

But she saw and heard it all again as the doctor stood at her bedside, waiting for an answer. The burning north tower. The falling bodies. The fiery explosion when the plane plowed through the south tower right in front of her. The carnage in the seventy-eighth-floor sky lobby. She saw it as clearly as if she were watching it on TV.

"Dave!" she cried out, trying to sit up. "Does Dave know I'm here? My husband is in the north tower. I have to go back and make sure he's all right. He'll be looking for me. He'll be worried. What time is it? How long have I been here?"

Members of the medical team held her down, and she saw them glance at one another. "The date is September sixteenth," the doctor said. "Sunday. You've been here since Tuesday."

September 16? What did he mean it was September 16? What was this doctor saying? It had only been moments ago that she was buried under the fire truck.

"You've been here for nearly a week," the doctor said. "If you give us a number for your husband, we'll try to reach him to let him know you're here."

"And my parents!" Tania cried. "My parents need to know where I am."

Tania's mother and father arrived while she was sleeping. When she opened her eyes and saw them, their faces red and swollen from crying, she began to sob, deep howling sobs that echoed up and down the halls of the intensive care unit. "You must save your strength," her mother said. "You nearly died. You're badly burned, and your arm had to be reattached. Sweet Tania. *Tu mama se encargara de ti.*" Mother will take care of you.

"Where is Dave?" Tania asked.

"Try to sleep," her mother said.

"Who's taking care of the dog, of Elvis?"

"We are."

As her parents kept vigil at her bedside, Tania went in and out of consciousness. Each time she woke, she asked for Dave. When her parents didn't answer, she was almost relieved. She wasn't sure how many days passed that way, with her asking for her husband, and her parents pretending not to hear. But one day she asked for Dave and her mother didn't turn away. She sat down beside her bed, took her hand, and slowly reviewed what was being replayed on television throughout the world:

Terrorists had flown two planes into the World Trade Center, her mother said, choosing each word as carefully as if it had the potential of a razor-sharp knife. The towers were gone, and hundreds of people were dead or still unaccounted for. Dave was among the missing.

The tears didn't come, not then. The ensuing weeks of burn treatment and physical therapy were agonizing for Tania. She had never suffered such excruciating pain, yet she went through the motions with the cold efficiency of a robot. The doctors had saved her arm but said that she would have only partial use of it, and the burn scars on the arm and her back would never fade completely. Tania could live with that. What she didn't tell anyone was that nightmares about Dave and things she had witnessed on the seventy-eighth floor made her afraid to go to sleep. Most nights, she lay awake, wishing she had died in the towers.

Tania wasn't sure what gave her the courage to keep going, except that sometimes she looked at her roommate and dared to hope for a miracle. The woman, Lauren Manning, an employee of the financial services firm Cantor Fitzgerald, had been critically burned in the north tower and was now in a medically induced coma, fighting for her life. Tania thought that Dave could be in a coma somewhere too.

The red and yellow leaves of fall had almost all dropped from the trees outside her hospital window when the doctor strode into her room one morning and said he had good news. She could go home in time to celebrate Thanksgiving with her family. Her mother jumped up and down like a child when she heard, and Tania pretended to be happy too, but the truth was that she dreaded going back to an empty apartment. For the past two months, she had convinced herself there was still hope that Dave was alive—maybe recovering in a hospital from serious injuries, or perhaps amnesia, so that even if he were able to contact her, he would have no way of knowing where she was. Once she got home, it wouldn't be as easy to imagine him trying to find her.

For the next few months, Tania slept away the days. At night, when everyone else was sleeping, she read everything she could about September 11 and studied photographs from that day, looking for any evidence of Dave. Even her mother, who stayed in New York to help

Lupe, the housekeeper, with the cooking and cleaning and tending to Elvis, couldn't convince her that Dave wasn't coming home. Finally, on March 25, 2002, six months after the towers fell, someone from the New York City coroner's office called to say that two fingerprints and a dental pattern had confirmed that Dave was dead. Tania accepted the news without shedding a tear. By then she felt completely empty and void of all feelings, happy or sad. What she knew was that she couldn't spend another night in that apartment, with so many reminders of happiness now lost forever. Dave wasn't coming home, there was no more pretending. She told Lupe to start packing up the place. They were leaving.

Tania took a spare two-bedroom on the eighteenth floor of the Westport in the Hell's Kitchen section of midtown. She had taken a quick look at the building and told the broker to draw up the papers. She was ready to move in. Living on Tenth Avenue would be a stark contrast to the patrician Upper East Side, and that's what she sought. Dave was gone, and she wanted to lock the memories of their life together away in the home they shared uptown. Her mother went back home. A year of lonely days and sleepless nights came and went.

As winter turned to spring in 2003, Tania sat at her kitchen window, staring at the budding trees along the avenue below, when she felt something stir inside her. She wasn't sure what it was, but it was a feeling, and, for the first time in more than a year, she almost felt like living again. Could there possibly be a new life after such interminable sorrow? She wasn't sure. But maybe it was worth trying to find out. A few days later, she was ready to make her move. She snapped open her laptop and Googled three words: "9/11 survivor help."

PART 2
2003

A SURVIVOR EMERGES

She logged in and introduced herself to a fledgling online support group in the early morning hours of May 13, 2003. Her words were vague and restrained, like so many survivors who had only just begun to confess publicly their months of silent suffering, the reasons for their ambiguity about reverence for the dead, and their guilt over being alive. They were just beginning to feel angry for being overlooked, the forgotten victims of the worst tragedy ever to embroider American soil, so they reached out to one another in the anonymous world of the Internet because no one else, not even their families, seemed to understand their hard feelings and lingering despair. They were, after all, the lucky ones. They had survived.

"I am only just starting to feel the consequences now despite having tried so hard to put it all behind me," she wrote in the online forum that Tuesday morning in May, twenty months after the terrorist attack. "I don't sleep, I see and hear the images and sounds, I'm moody, my stress and anxiety have skyrocketed, and a variety of other things. For so long I pretended to be OK that it is now hard to admit this is actually happening."

Manuel Chea sat at his kitchen table in Brooklyn, finishing his last cup of coffee before heading off to work, when he logged into the forum and saw the new post. Manny had joined the virtual support group three months earlier, and he often posted heartfelt messages about his struggles resulting from that terrible day downtown. He survived the attack, like so many had, by God's good grace, and, late at night, when he should have been sleeping, he thrashed around in his bed, fighting off nightmares and wondering why he had been spared when so many others died. The only things he ever came up with during those dark hours of sleeplessness were profound feelings of guilt and remorse, and recollections he wished he could forget.

September 11, 2001, had been primary election day in New York City, and Manny thought about casting his vote before going to his job at the World Trade Center. Instead he'd grabbed some breakfast at a fast-food restaurant and headed up to his office on the forty-ninth floor of the north tower, promising himself he would go to the polls that evening instead. It was eight o'clock when he sat down at his office desk. Manny knew this because he was a clock-watcher. Forty-six minutes later, he felt his building shake and tremble. What sounded to him like a sonic boom reverberated through the tower, and it swayed violently back and forth. "An earthquake," Manny thought, grabbing his backpack and running for the stairs.

It had taken Manny an hour to make it down forty-nine flights. The stairway was crowded with people, many of whom didn't seem to know what had happened, and he'd pushed his way past the slower ones, pausing only once to call his wife from an office on one of the low floors. The call hadn't gone through. He had been outside the north tower for only five minutes when the neighboring tower roared and came crashing down. Manny ran until his legs wouldn't carry him any farther, never looking back, finally making it home to Brooklyn in the late afternoon. The next day, he went back to work at a sister branch of his company on Long Island, as if nothing had ever happened. But he had never been able to get away from the regret he felt for not doing more to help his coworkers.

On the outside, Manny was his normal solid self. Inside, though, he was crumbling. At home, he was sullen and irritable. He was losing patience with his kids, and his once stable marriage felt shaky. One night Manny's wife told him that up until September 11, they were always on the same page. Now there was a gap between them that couldn't be filled. She called it "the 9/11 hole."

There was no such void between Manny and his fellow survivors. The tragedy was their bond, and they were attracted to one another like paper clips to a magnet. In the months following the attack, little attention was paid to the thousands of regular people who had made it out of the towers that morning. The focus of the massive media coverage and charitable outreach programs was first responders and families of the dead. Out of that seeming lack of empathy from the public grew a mounting sense of isolation on the part of the survivors, and many retreated into solitary cocoons of grief. For months, these vulnerable men and women quietly acquiesced to the role assigned them—that of inconsequential witnesses—until they could no longer deny their terminal misery and slowly began to seek out the only people who could understand: one another. Since Manny's coming out, he had confessed more of his feelings and fears to his faceless online comrades than he did to his own family and friends. In turn, he was always there for the other survivors when they needed a sympathetic ear. He read the new woman's confession with tears in his eyes.

"I think I need to talk to someone about this and tell my story, but I don't see how I will manage to do that," her post continued. "Going through it once was more than enough." The brief yet provocative message was signed simply, "God Bless, Tania."

Manny was compulsively punctual, but he didn't care if he was late to work that morning. He knew the angst of wanting desperately to talk about what happened in the towers but feeling too afraid to remember, or too unworthy to own the incessant suffering of having lived through it. The woman named Tania was clearly in distress, and he wanted her to know that she had come to the right place, where people understood the complexities of surviving such an unfathomable tragedy, and didn't pass judgment or assign degrees of grief. So he typed a short response to her post.

"Tania, I'm glad you joined," he wrote. "We are a relatively small group here, but we have a very good and strong group of people. We have encouraged one another in many ways, listened to each other, and supported each other as we have expressed what we've felt. Share with us your story when you are able to. :-) Manuel."

Within hours, other survivors posted words of welcome and encouragement for the newcomer.

"This group has really helped me, and I felt that this was a safe place for me to recount my experience," one survivor wrote. "Especially since I knew everyone here was feeling the same things I was."

"Hi, Tania," wrote another survivor. "I just joined the group too last night; I finally got up the courage. I feel so much like you do, like we all do, and right now I don't think I could tell what happened to me 'cause there's so much I don't remember. Only bits and pieces come back sometimes. I haven't been able to bring myself to even look at Manhattan since that day. Maybe when we both feel ready, we can help each other try."

Brendan Chellis was one of the original members of the survivors' group, having first posted in the forum nine months earlier, on the evening of August 19, 2002. Like many of the survivors, he had narrowly made it out of the towers. He resented being overlooked and misunderstood, and he politely complained about it in his inaugural post:

> We continue to be tortured by that day, yet it seems that nobody, even the people that are supposed to help us, understand what we are going through. We have all been through something horrible. We have seen things that people going to work on a beautiful day in September aren't supposed to see. Most of us at least one time that morning were convinced we were looking at our last seconds of life. But somehow we walked away (or more likely ran away). We watched thousands of people just like us die. Not on TV, but with our own eyes. We knew it was just a matter of chance that it was them and not us. And when other people got on with their lives, we suffered in obscurity with that day. We lived with the flashbacks, the depression, the anxiety, and especially the survivor guilt.

Since that first post, Brendan had come to terms with the fact that most people would never understand the plight of World Trade Center survivors, not without having walked in their shoes. He had done a lot of healing since his initial post the summer before, and he had helped dozens of others as they struggled with the consequences of that day. There were hundreds and probably thousands of others who were suffering as he'd been, but they didn't or couldn't reach out for help.

When Brendan saw Tania's post, he read in her words a certain despair that he recognized from his own early cries for help. He believed this was her last stab at seeing if she would ever be able to crawl out of the emotional quagmire that was drowning her, and he was determined to do what he could to help save her from herself.

"Tania," he wrote, "welcome to the group. We have been a little quiet lately, but hopefully having a new member will get people talking a little again. This group is a great place to be. When you get a chance, take a look at the old postings. (You have a lot of catching up to do!) Hopefully you'll see that a lot of the thoughts and emotions you have experienced (and thought you were alone with) have also been experienced by a lot of people in the group. I think that is what has been most reassuring to me. We all come from different backgrounds and went through different things on 9/11, yet we share the same emotional roller coaster since that day. It's good to know you are not alone in your feelings.

"Someday, if you're up for it, let us know your story. Otherwise, if you just want to share something, write it down and send it to the group. It helps as much to write things down as it does to hear from everyone else. I hope we can help you deal with some of the things you are going through."

Brendan wondered if he would ever hear from the woman named Tania again.

THE LIVING VICTIMS

Tania did return to the forum. During May and June of 2003, she posted short, grateful messages about how much the support from the other survivors was helping her to heal. In late June she agreed to join some of the others for a visit to the World Trade Center site, but she cancelled at the last minute, calling Brendan on his cell phone to say that she was sorry, but she wasn't ready to return there; she was still too fragile. Brendan described the visit on the forum the next day:

"The part of the day that I really liked was just being able to talk about 9/11 without worrying about making other people uncomfortable," he wrote. "For too long, I have felt like I have to keep my mouth shut whenever I am with other people because any talk about 9/11 is a sure conversation killer. But yesterday we all talked about our experiences, how it affected us, how we have been dealing with it, etc. At any time during the day, anybody could bring up what they were feeling, and sometimes we would just stop where we were and start talking about it."

An inherent tension existed between the survivors and the families of the men and women who'd lost their lives on 9/11. Family members were placed at the top of the hierarchy of grief, and some questioned the veracity of the survivors' distress—and even their right to grieve what had happened to them. After all, they were alive. They were the chosen ones. The survivors, on the other hand, were growing bitter about being misunderstood and overlooked. Because the survivors' forum was part of the World Trade Center United Families Group, an organization that had been formed first for families, and could be viewed by family members, the survivors who used it didn't feel comfortable with opening up about their suffering. But that restraint cracked in September of that year, on the second anniversary of the attack, when some of them were turned away from ground zero ceremonies.

For many of the survivors, the second anniversary memorial service was their first venture back to ground zero, and it had taken all of the courage they could muster to return. Yet when survivors were refused admission for not having the proper credentials to the invitation-only ceremony, the perceived slight unleashed a torrent of bitterness on the forum. As one survivor wrote:

> Yesterday morning early, I went down to the Trade Center site with my husband, and it was so sad, but what really got me was that of course the place was all barricaded, and there were people arriving for the memorial service who were being admitted, but, of course, not me. That always makes me feel both angry and very ashamed to be excluded like that. Like I committed some crime by surviving, and now I'm being punished by banishment. Like the authorities are saying to me, "You made your choice; you chose to survive, so now you forfeit all your claims to this place, to this event." It makes me positively suicidal. I feel like I just want to be erased, like I really deserve to be obliterated from the earth.

It was a sentiment shared by many of the other survivors: that in the expansive, complex dialogue of the September 11 story, they had been made invisible. "We are forgotten, and it's disgraceful," another survivor wrote. "I think we addressed this topic last year at the same time. I also wrote a letter to the *Daily News* editorial page about how we're forgotten and that we have to go along our merry way as if nothing ever happened! It's almost like cruel punishment, as you guys have said, for 'exiting the buildings alive.' They mourn the passing of their loved one(s) and can move on (which is the natural order of things) . . . We can't mourn any passing because we haven't physically lost someone, and if you haven't lost someone, you have no right to be at the Trade Center site and have no say as to what is built there. WE ARE LIVING VICTIMS."

After so many months of conceding their right to express grief, the survivors were prepared to claim their rightful place in the hierarchal order of suffering.

In late October Tania suggested that they split off from the United Families organization and start their own online support group, a place where they would be free to express even their rawest emotions without fear of judgment or rejection. "It's very easy to set up, and we could configure it as a private group so membership has to be approved by one of us," she posted on the morning of October 24. "All those in favor???????? I think it's important that we stick together."

Others in the group agreed that it was a good idea. At 12:59 p.m. that same afternoon, the World Trade Center Survivors Forum debuted online. The postings on the new site were immediately more intimate and revealing. People let down their guard, and real friendships formed quickly. The survivors could at last begin to purge themselves of the resentments they'd felt over being discounted, and even shunned, and bare their souls to one another.

The new group seemed to give Tania the impetus to begin finally opening up about herself, and, little by little, she shared snippets of her story. Then, late on a Saturday night in early November, she responded to another survivor's details of his experience in the south tower by recounting her harrowing moments in the seventy-eighth-floor sky lobby just before the plane plowed through it, and her long descent to safety.

She wrote:

I had started my way out and was on the sky lobby of the 78th floor waiting for the elevator when the plane hit. It was so crowded there. The elevators only took 60 secs down to the lobby, but that day, whether true or not, they seemed to be running too slow. Everybody was pushing trying to get into the elevators. I remember this one guy who yelled, "Ladies, this is not the *Titanic*. It's not women and children first." Shortly after that, someone yelled that there was a plane coming. We heard the roaring noise from the jet, then there was a deafening explosion, and a fireball ripped through the lobby. I find it very hard to talk about what happened afterward.

"Do you remember any injured women walking down past you on the stairs?" she asked the other survivor. "I wonder if we crossed paths that day."

Two days later, Tania shared more details of her story. She wrote about grabbing the shirts of people who no longer needed them and wrapping them around her burned and bleeding arms and legs, and crawling over dead people and through pools of blood looking for an escape. "Others around me were getting quiet, I knew they were dying, and I didn't want to be one of them," she wrote. "The fire conditions were getting worse, and air was getting scarce. My lungs were burning inside. I kept thinking about my life, my family, my fiancé, about our wedding."

She told of stumbling upon the dying man who put his wedding ring in her hand and asked her to give it to his wife, and of being rescued by the man with the red bandanna covering his mouth. "He said he had found the stairs." And she revealed the tragic loss of her beloved Dave. She said that she never would have made it out of the building if it hadn't been for her thoughts of him and their impending wedding at the Plaza.

"I wanted to wear that white dress and swear my love for him in front of friends and family. I wanted to have his children," she wrote. "He was in the other tower . . . I didn't know then that he would not survive. I believe today that he stopped to give me the strength to get out of there on his way to heaven. . . . I was one of the last people out of tower 2."

Her story was jaw dropping. Not only had she miraculously escaped from what looked like a certain and terrible death but she had also lost the man she loved. Within days, word of the new survivor and her unparalleled account of survival and loss had spread throughout the survivor community.

The unknown blogger had taken her first steps to becoming the face of one of the most tragic chapters in the history of the United States.

A MEETING OF
THE MINDS

Gerry Bogacz lived through the 1993 bombing of the World Trade Center, and he was on the eighty-second floor of the north tower on September 11 when American Airlines Flight 11 slammed into the building. A private, guarded man, Bogacz shared the dramatic details of what he went through that day only with his wife and daughter, his closest friends, and a handful of survivors he had come to know in the two years since the attack. Indeed, when he finally put pen to paper to write down his memories of that life-changing time, he preceded the thirty-six-page narrative with a note:

> This is an account of my experiences during the attack and its aftermath, which I've written so that family and friends will have a sense of what happened. Recording my experiences and sharing them on a limited basis will help me and those closest to me to better comprehend what transpired. In addition, this information will hopefully shed some light on the experiences of the others who were in the buildings that day. I offer this account for them also, so that any readers will know a little more about what happened to them and to me in the buildings and afterward.

As planning director for the New York Metropolitan Transportation Council, Bogacz had been facing a typically hectic schedule when he arrived at the World Trade Center on the morning of September 11. He had gotten to his office early to catch up on phone calls and emails before the first of a series of scheduled meetings began. By eight thirty, he was sitting at his computer, reading and responding to emails from the day before. At one point, a member of his staff popped in with the agenda for the nine o'clock meeting. After he left, Bogacz put the finishing touches on a letter to a local newspaper, and then walked down the hall to visit another associate.

The coworker's office offered a spectacular view to the north, and, on that cloudless morning, Bogacz could see well past the Empire State Building in midtown, all the way up the Hudson River to the Bronx and into Westchester and Rockland counties. As he stood there, admiring the panorama and chatting with his colleague, he sensed a sudden, subtle change in the air pressure—"as if air were being forced into the building," he would say later.

The pressure change was accompanied by a high-pitched whirring sound. Bogacz stopped talking, and he could see from his colleague's crinkled brow that he, too, had sensed something curious. Before either of them could say anything, the building was rocked by what Bogacz described as "a titanic explosion." The north tower lurched violently toward the southern end of the island and then fiercely snapped back in place. People in the office grabbed desktops, chairs— anything they could hang onto—to keep from falling over.

After a moment of terrified silence, Bogacz saw an enormous chunk of debris plunge past the eighty-second-floor windows. Somewhere in the back of his mind, he thought that the huge, fall-ing mass could be a missile. That was when the urgency of the situation kicked in.

Bogacz's mind raced back to February 26, 1993, when terrorists exploded a truck bomb in the basement of the building. Back then, he had evacuated into a smoke-filled stairwell, and more than half of the trip down had been made in complete darkness. It had taken nearly four hours to get out of the building that day, and the stress had taken its toll. This time seemed far worse, and he wondered if the tower was stable enough to withstand whatever had happened. Or was it about to fall down?

"Hit the stairs!" Bogacz shouted to his coworkers. What he remem-bered happening next was a group of them moving through the office suite toward the main corridor. In his haste to get out of the office, he stumbled on a colleague who was crawling out of his cubicle and me-chanically jumped over him. The impulse to escape was overpowering, absolute. Looking back over his shoulder, Bogacz saw others from his office beginning to move, and he picked up his step. The fear of being trapped in a crowded stairwell, as he had been eight years before, was all-consuming. When he finally reached the door leading out to the corridor, he stopped short. The hallway was thick with heavy, black smoke. "Don't go out there," he told himself. "You don't know what that smoke means." But the hall was the only route to the stairs.

The sound of a colleague's voice snapped Bogacz out of his inde-cisiveness. "Get to the stairwell now!" the man shouted. Impulsively, Bogacz pushed frantically through the office door and dove into the smoky hall. Whatever was out there was certain to be in his office soon, so what was there to lose? The entrance to stairway A was only a few feet away. As he turned into the stairway, he was showered with a surge of radiant heat. An oily, burning electrical smell filled the air. At least this time, unlike in 1993, only trickles of people were on the stairs, and the lights were still working.

Bogacz headed down the stairs with a few of his colleagues trailing him. "Everybody stay calm and keep moving!" he shouted, more out of his growing anxiety than a nudge to the people going down. But they did need to move fast, away from the fire burning above them, before the building fell. A few flights down, Bogacz overheard some-one in the stairwell say that a plane had crashed into the building. He had often seen planes flying over the towers from his office. An acci-dent certainly wasn't out of the question.

With each floor, more people entered the stairwell, but they still moved at a decent pace. Bogacz had gone down thirty floors when he felt heaviness in his chest and his legs go rubbery. He feared he was having a heart attack, but he forced himself to focus on one step at a time. Smoke was creeping into the stairwell from underneath the doors, and with every floor, the temperature seemed to rise. He began to feel trapped, the way he had in the suffocating stairwell after the 1993 bombing.

At the forty-third floor, a man wearing street clothes was holding open the door, wordlessly beckoning Bogacz and the others to leave the stairs. Like soldiers following a command, they all filtered into the forty-third-floor lobby and joined a crowd waiting to get into the emergency stairwell on the opposite side of the building. With so many bodies jockeying for position, Bogacz found himself caught in a bottleneck. Perhaps the man holding the door knew something they didn't, but the stairway they had just come from seemed like a better choice. His anxiety swelled.

Standing there, he noticed a small bank of elevators. Smoke leached out from behind their closed doors. It was too much. Without a word, he broke away from the line and bolted back across the lobby to stairway A. Maybe it was a dead end, but he had to keep moving. Some of his colleagues followed, and soon they were back in the original stairway, headed down. But their progress was short lived.

A few floors down, they hit a logjam of people. As had happened in 1993, the narrow stairwell was clogged, and every movement forward was interrupted by agonizing periods of standing still. Only people with injuries were allowed to pass, and most of them were badly burned. Someone would yell "Injured!" and everyone moved to the right to let them get by. It had been that way with the wounded the last time too. Bogacz remembered how troubled he had been afterward, when he'd read accounts of people assisting each other down the stairs and questioned why he had been too focused on his own escape to help anyone else. Now he knew the answer. The urge to get out of the building was overpowering. He looked up the stairs and saw a burned woman slowly making her way down. Her face was red and swollen, and she was moaning in pain. Someone shouted, "Injured person!" and everyone moved to the side to let the woman and her escort squeeze past. The brief delay was agonizing and Bogacz struggled not to panic. Time seemed to stand still until the procession finally began to move again. With a clear path ahead, he was able to descend past the fortieth floor and through the thirties fairly quickly. Somewhere in the twenties, he encountered a group of firefighters making its way up the stairs. The firefighters stepped aside, allowing civilians to go by. The stairwell was getting hotter, and Bogacz felt sweat dripping into his eyes. He pushed closer to the person ahead of him, as if by doing so he could get out of the building faster. His skin prickled with fear. Finally, after what had seemed like an eternity, he was down.

Bogacz moved across the main lobby toward the turnstiles, where uniformed emergency workers were guiding people to safety. Out on the street, it was chaos. People flooded out of the towers, and police barked orders. "Keep moving!" "Don't look back!" Bogacz did as he was told and ran off.

A few blocks away, he turned to look at the buildings. They had disappeared inside a giant plume of smoke and debris. He thought about his family. Surely they thought he was dead, but he had no way to call them. His cell phone was in his bag up on the eighty-second floor, and it probably wouldn't have worked anyway. He thought about his office. He was certain it was in ruins. They had probably lost everything. He thought about the towers and how they would look when the flames were extinguished, and he wondered how long it would take to repair them. Part of him felt disconnected from what had just happened. He felt almost as if he had observed the disaster from a distance rather than lived through it.

Eight hours later, Bogacz was finally back home with his family in the Bronx. The towers were gone. Thousands were dead or missing. He stripped off his jacket and trousers and sat on the edge of his bed, feeling cold and numb. Sleep wouldn't come, not that night, or the next, or the night after that. He would soon learn that three of his colleagues died in the tower. The coworkers who had been with him on the stairs were caught in the congestion and barely made it out of the building with their lives.

In the months after the attack, Bogacz suffered severe bouts of depression and stress, but most of all, guilt. He quietly berated himself for not staying in his office longer to make sure that his coworkers had all evacuated, and he second-guessed his decision to flee as quickly as he had. One day he passed an impromptu memorial outside a church near where the towers had stood and stopped to read the messages. They were from people all over the world. Before moving on, he left his own message: "I escaped from the World Trade Center on September 11th. I am very sorry for those who did not." Those two sentences summed up the whole, awful experience. Tears stung his eyes as he walked away. A year later, he was still taking antidepressants to be able to get through the days and still looking for ways to redress his survival.

At the same time that others were coming together in the online forum, Bogacz was floating to fellow survivors the idea of a support group. After work on February 26, 2003, a group of a dozen gathered at the Cedar Tavern in the West Village to talk it over. They discovered that they had all begun thinking about reaching out to other survivors at about the same time and decided that was significant. If they had all been suffering with the same feelings of angst and isolation, surely there were other survivors who were still struggling and needed the same sense of belonging. Toasting to a better future, the group clinked glasses that night and promised to forge ahead. That August, Bogacz sent out a solicitation email to a wide net of professionals, and, by word of mouth, news of the support group spread.

On September 23, 2003, Bogacz presided over the inaugural meeting of the survivors' group in the basement of St. Andrew's Roman Catholic Church in Lower Manhattan. The group adopted a statement of purpose, which was to address "the high probability that large numbers of survivors—those placed at immediate risk of injury or death during the attacks—have had their lives significantly disrupted and altered by the experience and, as a result, continued to face stress, disorientation, and significant levels of grief, guilt, and helplessness in the aftermath of the attacks."

A second meeting was scheduled for November 19 at Trinity Church on Wall Street. It was then, as the members of the fledgling group shared a potluck supper in the church hall, in the shadow of the former World Trade Center, that someone mentioned a survivor named Tania Head and her incredible account of survival and loss. Bogacz was smitten with the story.

"I want to meet her," he said.

PART 3

2004

A PRESENCE

All eyes were on her as she walked into the meeting at 520 Eighth Avenue in Manhattan on January 28, 2004. None of them had ever seen her, but they all knew who she was. She was Rubenesque and not conventionally pretty, but her cheeks were apple red, her dark eyes sparkled when she smiled, and she was well turned out in her tailored, moss-colored pantsuit and Rolex watch.

What struck everyone had nothing to do with her appearance, though. She had a presence. It was undeniable, even mesmerizing. And her story, well, it would have been unbelievable if it hadn't been so beyond belief. Some of them didn't feel worthy to be in the room with her.

Of course, the anticipation of her arrival had been spine tingling. It was all any of them could talk about for days before. In the few short weeks since she'd posted her amazing account of bravery and heartbreak online, Tania had become a legend in the awakening survivor community. She was the ubersurvivor. So when she walked into the meeting, it felt to the other two dozen or so men and women there as if a celebrity had entered the room.

This was the survivors' group's first meeting at the place called September Space, a suite on the eleventh floor of an office building at the corner of West Thirty-Sixth Street in the garment district. It had been designated by the nonprofit organization World Cares specifically for 9/11-related activities and would become the group's home base.

Gerry Bogacz had invited Tania. The two began an email friendship shortly after he'd heard about her, and they'd done a lot of messaging and talking on the phone over the holidays. There came a point, with each of the survivors, when family members could no longer provide the emotional sustenance needed to keep going. How many times could a husband or a wife be expected to listen to the same dismal memories, the same angry rants, the same irrational confessions of guilt and shame? How could they possibly understand what it was like to live through something that most people couldn't even imagine, or the conflicting repercussions of surviving such a cataclysmic nightmare?

Bogacz had reached the point where he felt as if his family couldn't relate to him anymore, or maybe it was the other way around. He was a lone man stranded in a foreign place where no one understood the language he spoke, and he was tired of trying to explain how he got there and why he wasn't able to go back to where he'd been. The trouble was that he no longer even recognized the man he'd been on September 10, 2001, and sometimes he wondered if his post-9/11 self was even compatible with his former life. In Tania he had discovered someone who truly understood, a person who had been in a darker place than he was, worse than any of the other survivors, and had somehow found her way back to the light.

He was surprised when he saw her. From their email exchanges and phone conversations, Bogacz had formed a mental picture of Tania, and he was expecting someone different, someone with a face that matched the honeyed voice with a hint of a Spanish accent. It didn't matter what she looked like, of course, but it had just taken him aback at first. He walked toward her with his hand outstretched, eager to introduce himself, and the moment they greeted each other, hugging and patting each other on the back, he knew they would be good friends. Tania was warm and unassuming and a little bit shy. And when people surrounded her, competing for a moment of her time, she seemed comfortable and responsive but far from caught up in all of the attention.

At six o'clock, Bogacz called the meeting to order. After a moment of silence for the people who perished in the towers, everyone took a place around a long, rectangular conference table. Tania sat quietly at first as they discussed ideas for the structure and mission of the group. But as the meeting wore on, she seemed to relax, and she summoned a few of her thoughts and opinions about ways to get the group off the ground.

By the end of the evening, they had settled on a name—the World Trade Center Survivors' Network—and drafted a mission statement that began, "The Survivors' Network seeks to provide a forum for personal contact between survivors as a means to empower them both to deal with the circumstances of the aftermath of the attacks and find renewed purpose in that aftermath. The network can also function as a place for people to go and get survivors' perspectives and as a conduit for the common thoughts of survivors."

The seed planted by Bogacz nearly a year earlier had sprung its first blossom. They were officially a group with a name, a direction, and an ambitious long-term agenda. They would begin by identifying as many of the people who had survived the attack on the towers as they could—a challenge because the number that survived was somewhere in the thousands. Then their job would be finding ways to facilitate the needs of their forgotten comrades. Ultimately, the survivors would need to find a common voice to finally be recognized as part of the 9/11 community and have a say in the important decisions about the rebuilding and memorials at the World Trade Center site.

It was time to move forward. But the next step had chinks that, up till then, had proved insurmountable.

In the two years and four months since the destruction of the towers, and life as they'd known it, the survivors had never been permitted private access to ground zero the way that family members and first responders had. If they chose to go to the site to pay their respects to the dead or to spend a moment reflecting on that life-changing morning, they were expected to tough it out like every other visitor and wade through throngs of tourists with their fanny packs and cameras, and past the dozens of vendor carts with 9/11 baseball caps and postcards with the towers before and after the attack—only to be stopped at the tall metal fencing that surrounded the trade center grounds. Bogacz and every other founding member of his group tried repeatedly to arrange a private tour for survivors to visit the footprint of the towers, but the powers within the Port Authority of New York and New Jersey had always rebuffed their requests—another indication that the survivors were invisible.

The number one item on the network's agenda was to facilitate a Survivors' Day at the site, a time when only they would be permitted inside the fence. "This would provide survivors the opportunity to remember, find solace, and to move forward in the healing process," the group wrote in the meeting minutes. It would also go a long way toward lending credibility to the new network and drawing in other survivors. But how to do it? Everyone agreed to come up with strategies for discussion at the next gathering.

After the meeting adjourned, Bogacz and Tania walked two blocks through the foot of snow that blanketed the city to the twenty-four-hour Tick Tock Diner, which was located across from Penn Station and served breakfast all day. Over multiple cups of coffee, they talked about their lives since 9/11 and how lonely it was being a survivor. Tania told him that for nearly two years afterward, she had rarely left her apartment. She had been stuck in a debilitating depression, was unable to return to her job, and had gained a lot of weight. She still couldn't go to sleep without leaving on a light. One day she woke up and decided that enough was enough. If she was ever going to heal, she had to crawl outside of herself and do something to help others. Bogacz was struck by Tania's optimism and kindheartedness. After all she'd been through, she was still able to smile and laugh, and she encouraged him to do the same.

At one point, Tania suggested that her online support group merge with the Survivors' Network. There was power in numbers, she said. One comprehensive organization would have more political might than small, fractured groups, and that meant reaching larger numbers of survivors. She said that she was ready and willing to put in as much time as it took to pull it all together, even if it meant using her own money and spending less time at her job at Merrill Lynch. Bogacz agreed that it sounded like a good idea, and he was convinced it could work. With their strong management backgrounds, they could accomplish a lot together, he said, and hopefully some of her optimism and energy would rub off on him in the process.

The truth was that Bogacz was grateful to have a partner who was willing to listen to his cares and concerns, and who was motivated to advocate on behalf of all survivors. There was so much hard work ahead to get the survivors the acknowledgment they deserved, and he knew it would take more time and energy than he had to give. And, he thought, if this brave woman had been able to avenge the tragedy by turning her misery into action—returning to her career in the financial industry, lending support to a 9/11 families group by volunteering her time to help widows like her cope with their feelings of loss, and now coming out in a snowstorm for her fellow survivors— there was no telling what she could do for the network.

The two finished their last cups of coffee and shook hands before saying good night. But before he went his way and she went hers, Tania promised that she would set to work the minute she got back to her Hell's Kitchen apartment. She wasn't a good sleeper anyway.

"I'll be in touch," she said, shaking the snow from her scarf.

"Good luck," Bogacz said before heading down to the subway.

Tania went home and first sent notes to her survivor friends telling them of the new network. She then stayed up late into the night figuring out how to get in touch with survivors of the 1995 bombing of the Alfred P. Murrah Federal Building in Oklahoma City, where 168 people died, including 19 children in day care, to find out how they had established themselves. By the time she finally dropped into bed, she'd sent an email introducing herself to Richard Williams, a survivor of the Oklahoma City bombing, and another to Bob Schutz, a friend she'd met on the forum who happened to be the World Trade Center site supervisor, asking for advice about how to get that private trip down to ground zero that no one had been able to arrange.

Six weeks later, on March 17, Tania sent an email to the network with astonishing news. Where everyone else had failed, she had succeeded in getting the private visit to the site that they so desperately wanted. "I have arranged a visit to ground zero for WTC survivors," she wrote. "During the visit, those of you who are up to it will have the opportunity to descend to the bottom of the pit. I realize many of you still find it hard to go to the site, so please think about this carefully. Tania."

On May 7 she followed up with another message detailing the arrangements for the tour. Everything was set. They were on for the following Friday morning, she said. The supervisor of the site, a friend with whom she had been working quietly to make the visit happen, was putting himself out on a limb by accommodating them, and he had asked that they keep it low key, with no fanfare or media coverage. It was a small price to pay for such a huge victory. Many of the survivors had barely escaped from the towers with their lives, and they had hardly come away unscathed. Yet this was the first time since the tragedy that someone in authority had recognized that they had a rightful tie to the place, and it went a long way toward legitimizing their feelings of anguish and deep sorrow.

Tania was clearly excited about giving the others the news. Before signing off on her message, she wrote, "We're only a week away from the big day!"

RETURN TO GROUND ZERO

The day of the tour debuted with a brilliant yellow sun embellished on a bare, blue sky—the mirror image of September 11. As the group of twenty or so survivors passed through the tall, mesh fencing surrounding the missing twin towers—a fence that had come to symbolize the divide between those who belonged and everyone else—Gerry Bogacz felt oddly as if he had come home.

Tania led the way into the urban wasteland, sixteen ruinous acres in the heart of the world's premier financial center that had tragically come to be known as ground zero. This was her stage, and no one was about to begrudge her the lead role. Tania was stoic walking in. She had been to the site more than a year earlier, she said, with one of the first family tours. This time she would experience it not as a bereft widow whose husband had died there but as they would: as someone trying to cope with the battle scars of surviving.

The small group of survivors straggled down the concrete access ramp leading from street level to the towers' footprints, a pair of giant tetragons that had been built where bedrock begins, six stories underground, to support what were to be the world's tallest buildings. No one spoke as they walked the long ramp to the sacred soil below. It hadn't been long since the last of the body parts were pulled from the site. Tania picked up a handful of dirt and let it slip through her fingers. Like so many others who descended the ramp to the "floor," some survivors felt what they believed to be the presence of the people who had lost their lives there. To some it felt like a warm breeze swirling up from the basin. Others sensed the air turn thick, as if with an oppressive kind of sadness, as they reached hallowed ground. Tania described the same sensation of comfort she'd experienced that morning in the south tower, when she felt Dave guiding her to safety. He was there with her, she said. She could feel him.

In two months, on the Fourth of July, the city would sink the cornerstone for the replacement Freedom Tower in the northwest corner of ground zero—twenty tons of polished Adirondack granite with an inscription that read: "To honor and remember those who lost their lives on September 11th, 2001 and as a tribute to the enduring spirit of freedom—July Fourth, 2004." It was a symbol of the city's resolve to rebuild. Now there was just a dank hole with pockmarked concrete walls and a red-clay floor covered with gravel. Here and there, a weed poked through the grit. Life renewed itself even in places darkened by death.

The survivors stood in a circle, each lost in his or her private thoughts. They had knots in their throats and tears in their eyes. Looking toward the heavens, Bogacz was suddenly struck by the vast interlude of empty space in the landscape where the towers had been. Someone once called it a hole in the city's heart. It was an apt description, he thought. That gap was once occupied by an architectural marvel, thriving with people from all over the city and all over the world. Now it was air. It was still hard to grasp. He looked over at Tania, who was comforting another survivor. She had suffered a constellation of misfortune that would have shattered most people. Yet rather than submitting to her heartbreak, she had turned it into a crusade to help everyone else who was suffering. "What an amazing woman," he thought.

In some ways, her motivation was more selfish than selfless, Tania would say later. Helping others was a way to save herself; to hold onto her sanity, her will to live. For two years after the attack, she barely slept at night and she was still afraid to close her eyes. Most of the time when she did, she saw crashing planes and mangled bodies. Debilitating panic attacks and constant thoughts of dying plagued her. Sometimes her guilt—for leaving some of her coworkers behind; for not having coffee with Dave that morning, which might have spared his life; for saving herself—made her wish she was dead.

Her sunny disposition and easy smile were a mask. "Make-believe," she said. She still had days when someone lit a candle, and she was back on the seventy-eighth floor, crawling through flames and over dead bodies. There were still times when a plane flew overhead, and her fear was so intense that she blacked out—once even awakening to find herself sprawled on the side of the West Side Highway downtown. She was broken, and she didn't have the glue to piece herself back together. So she pretended to be okay, and she made sure every minute of every day was filled so that she didn't have to think or feel. It was the only way she knew how to cope. And if by helping herself she helped the other survivors, she was glad.

The group members remained for an hour or so, paying their respects to the dead, remembering the day that changed their lives, and beginning to let go of pent-up feelings and emotions that could be released only by being there. Some left flowers and cards. Tania left a letter for Dave, saying how much she missed him and loved him, and how all that sustained her were thoughts of their time together and what life might have been.

The visit to ground zero had gone a long way to helping the survivors take the next step toward the rest of their lives, whatever that was. Years afterward, a young woman named Carrie Coen Sullivan, who had worked in the south tower for only a month when it was struck, would remember the visit as the turning point in her healing—the singular event that gave her the freedom to start to forgive herself for surviving and think about living again. Walking out of the site, she felt a sense of peace that she hadn't known since before September 11. It brought her to tears.

Tania led the procession all the way up the ramp and back to the street, through the tall fence that separated those with a rightful claim to the tragedy and the rest of the world. The survivors were no longer outsiders looking in. They finally belonged. Before going their separate ways that day, they crowded around her, hugging her and thanking her for what she had done.

Tania just smiled.

Afterward, she wrote to her new confidante about the experience.

Richard Williams was a survivor of the Oklahoma City disaster nine years earlier, when a disgruntled antigovernment army veteran named Timothy McVeigh parked a Ryder truck full of explosives outside the Alfred P. Murrah Federal Building and detonated it. Williams was trapped beneath piles of debris, with only his left arm showing, when a rescuer discovered him and carried him out of the rubble. Critically injured, he'd spent two years recovering from both the physical and emotional trauma. He'd eventually turned his torment into action by becoming involved in survivors' programs and memorial planning in Oklahoma City. After weeks of sharing nearly daily emails, and some of their innermost thoughts, Williams and Tania became friends.

"The site visit with fellow survivors was very hard," she wrote to Richard. "We all went down to the pit together and brought flowers and cards for our friends and colleagues who didn't make it. It was the first time survivors went to the site since 9/11, and seeing their pain was heart wrenching. After the visit, most of us went to September Space, and we sat around in a circle with a counselor and we described how we felt. It was amazing. It was the first time most of us opened our hearts and feelings to each other face to face. I was fascinated at seeing how even the guys I thought were the toughest had so much inside of them that they needed to share with the rest of us."

The visit, Tania wrote, made her grieve for Dave even more, if that were possible. "Next week I'll be going down to the town where Dave grew up," she wrote. "They are dedicating a garden for him and the four other victims from NC who died on 9/11. Although I'm glad they're doing something like this and recognizing him, it's going to be so hard to see his name etched in stone. I know I'm going to cry my eyes out during the ceremony and for days to come. My parents and some of my brothers will be there too. I know Dave would have liked that and would be glad we still all remember him and are as close to his family as ever. I love going to his house and going through the albums of his childhood with his mom. That has become a tradition, and it's a moment she and I share every time I visit them."

In closing, Tania wrote about the recent kidnapping and murder of an American hostage in Saudi Arabia by Al Qaeda. She didn't want to feel hatred toward anyone, but forgiving the murderers who had taken Dave and continued to kill innocent people was beyond her capability. "I miss him so much these days and feel I need him more than ever," she wrote. "The beheading of Paul Johnson was so hard for me. It's the same people who did this to us, and they are still free to hurt even more people." In another email to Williams at around that time, she complained bitterly about a man posting on the forum who, it had turned out, feigned being a 9/11 survivor. In her eyes, that, too, was unforgivable.

She wrote:

Until now, our Yahoo group has had the policy to accept anyone who applied because we trusted in people's good faith. I mean who would want to fake being a World Trade Center survivor, right? God knows how much I've been through and this guy is just here for the attention or whatever sick reason. He's reading everything I write, which is quite personal stuff because we all pour out our most intimate thoughts.

Well, after I found out about this guy, I immediately wrote to the other moderators of the online group and asked them to ban him and to change our acceptance policy. I know you've told me you had some problems with fakes before. So, yes, at some point, we're going to sit down and establish a policy to define survivors. I think, the way things are now, there's a slim chance it will happen again, but we need to be prepared.

A FRIEND IN NEED

Linda Gormley felt her heart hammering in her chest as she sat in the back of the crowded room. It was her first survivors' meeting, and it had taken everything she had to get herself there. Linda was single and in her thirties, a pale-skinned blonde with signature bright red lips. She was pretty and personable, but as fragile as glass and willing to do almost anything for people to like her. She didn't know where she fit into the 9/11 community, or even if there was a place in the chain of suffering for people like her. Others had lost loved ones in the attack, or had near-death experiences, or tales of narrow escapes. Linda hadn't lost anyone, and she wasn't in the towers that day. But she had seen things so awful from the sidewalk that, for months afterward, she would drink until the images finally blurred into oblivion. Now she was sober and grappling with those crushing, impeccable memories.

The young woman had attempted to validate her struggle by attending an anniversary ceremony at ground zero as a volunteer for the American Red Cross, handing out tissues and flowers to family members and rescue workers. She felt compelled to be in the presence of the families, as if studying their grief would help her feel entitled to her own. As it was, the ceremony had the opposite effect. Seeing the grief etched on the faces of people who had lost husbands and wives and parents and children made her feel more like a voyeur than a victim. She just didn't belong.

She questioned whether she was worthy of being in the company of the survivors either, for that matter. Even if they did accept her, she was pretty sure that she wasn't ready to bare her emotions to a roomful of strangers. As she sat there, crossing and recrossing her legs, waiting for the meeting to begin, Linda debated whether to stay or go home. Then she saw Tania.

Tania swept into the meeting room with her summer floral skirt flowing behind her and a white blouse pressed to perfection, smiling and laughing as if she had the world on a string. The way she carried herself said that she was somebody, Linda thought to herself. People didn't learn that kind of poise. They were born to it. Watching the others interact with her, Linda was reminded of a scene from *The Wizard of Oz* in which Glinda the Good Witch summons the Munchkins ("Come out, come out, wherever you are!"), and they flock to her, all happy and bubbly. "Who *is* that girl?" she wondered. And as if having read Linda's thoughts, the woman beside her leaned over and whispered, "That's Tania."

Linda knew something about Tania. She had met her online a few weeks earlier when she joined the survivors' forum. In fact, it had been Tania who responded to her first post, suggesting that she come to a meeting of the Survivors' Network. She was vaguely aware that Tania had escaped from the south tower but knew little else. So she watched, fascinated, as one person after the next jockeyed to get a word with Tania.

One woman introduced herself as Amanda Ripley, a reporter for *Time* magazine. Ripley was in the process of interviewing survivors for a story. In her travels, she'd met another survivor who told her she should speak to Tania; that Tania's story was bigger than all of the others. The other survivor, acting as a go-between, had approached Tania about doing the interview, and she agreed to speak to Ripley at some point; she just wasn't sure when she could fit it into her schedule.

Ripley, having heard that Tania was willing to talk to her, had come to the meeting simply to formally introduce herself, leave her business card, and perhaps set up a date to meet. But she'd barely had the chance to say her piece when the others stepped in. Tania was having a bad day, they said, rebuking the reporter for approaching her. Ripley was whisked out of the meeting and escorted from the building. By the time the evening was over, Linda was completely intrigued and wanted to know more about the special survivor.

Linda didn't approach Tania that night, except to briefly introduce herself, but she did race home to scope her out online. She didn't have to look further than the group forum archives to find what she needed to know. She was stunned to read Tania's powerful account from the previous November about her life-and-death escape from one tower, and losing her husband in the other. A more recent post, written just before Linda had discovered the forum that spring, was heart wrenching.

"Today I got a promotion at work, and I still don't know why," Tania wrote. "Most of the time, my mind is miles away. I relive over and over the moments I shared with Dave, my fiancé who died in the north tower. After I heard about the promotion, I had this urge to call the store where the wedding dress I never got to wear was being stored and told them to go ahead and donate it to charity. This is a big step for me. It's been accumulating dust for 2½ years . . . and it's time. Tania."

Sitting at her home computer, trying to take it all in, Linda felt as if she couldn't possibly attend another survivors' meeting or even post on the forum anymore. If Tania was the definition of a survivor, how could she deign to put herself in that category? She didn't even deserve to share the same air with her. She wrote that in an email to Tania that night, and, within minutes, Tania responded most graciously, the way that she did with others who had expressed similar sentiments. Of course she deserved to be part of the group, Tania wrote Linda. Everyone's story was of equal importance and value. They weren't competing for best survivor, ha-ha. No one's experience was any more or less compelling than anyone else's. They were all wounded souls who needed to stick together. She ended her note with "Warm regards, Tania."

The next meeting coincided with the *Time* magazine story hitting the newsstands, and everyone was chattering about it when Linda arrived at September Space. As it turned out, Tania had been interviewed for the story after all. Accompanied by another survivor for moral support, she had met with Ripley for coffee a few days after the last meeting. She did it, she told the others, certainly not for herself—she didn't even like reporters much—but because she recognized an opportunity for the survivors to have a national platform. Tania was glowing. "Not bad, huh?" she said, holding up her copy.

Linda's admiration for Tania intensified even more when she read the magazine story. Not only was it one of the very first articles to address survivors and the complex issues with which they still struggled three years after the tragedy, but this brave woman—despite all she endured and all she lost—had been instrumental in delivering the message.

Ripley wrote:

New York City is engaged in America's first experiment with a mass-casualty disaster that has no end point. Manhattan residents say they are using more cigarettes, alcohol, and marijuana since 9/11, and they remain worried about new attacks, according to research by the New York Academy of Medicine.

But as with Vietnam vets, the ability of New Yorkers to process a trauma depends largely on how close people were to the carnage.

Still, psychologists say the most overexposed—and under recognized—victims may be the nearly 20,000 New Yorkers who walked, ran, and crawled through smoke, fire, and body parts to escape the buildings. "People cannot understand. We saw things," says Tania Head, who was injured while evacuating. "We had to make life-or-death decisions. The higher the floor, the more lonely you were. I can't get rid of my fear that it's going to happen again."

The magazine story validated what survivors had felt for so long. September 11 was a national tragedy, and everyone wanted a piece of it, to connect with it in some fundamental way. It was human nature to want to be part of the "big story," and there were few bigger in contemporary history than the fall of what Minoru Yamasaki, the architect of the World Trade Center, once called "a living symbol of man's dedication to world peace." How many people said things like "I was in the towers the week before the attack," or "I knew someone who knew someone who was there that day," or "My cousin's brother-in-law saw the towers fall," or "It could have been me"?

Linda sat there thinking that she would have given anything to loiter on the fringes of the disaster like most of the rest of the world. Instead she was sinking under the weight of untoward memories of that hellish morning. She—all of them—had been "overexposed" to the wretchedness of it all, and then they were expected to carry on as usual, as if they had been sitting in their living rooms somewhere in the Midwest, watching it on TV. Maybe now, people would begin to understand who the survivors were: anonymous men and women who were damaged by unimaginable trauma.

They thanked Tania for that. They stood and applauded her, and she giggled, curtsied, and took a deep bow. Linda looked at her with awe. "This woman runs the group," she said to herself. "She's in charge, and she has everyone spellbound. I know who I want to be friends with. I want to be in the center of things too." But Linda's attraction to Tania was more than just about gaining status in the group. She was inspired by Tania's courage and resilience. After all she had suffered, she was able to put back the pieces of her life, and she was helping them to put back the pieces of theirs. Linda wanted that kind of character. She had been mired in an artificial fog for so long that she didn't even know the real Linda anymore. "I want to be like her," Linda told herself as she watched Tania relish the attention she was getting. "This is the life I want to live."

Linda began looking for opportunities to connect with Tania. Her chance came when the survivors' group took a trip to the Museum of Natural History on Central Park West for a lighthearted scavenger hunt. It would be their first social outing together, and everyone looked a little awkward. Tania seemed a little standoffish at first. Linda followed her to the coat check and tried to make small talk without much luck. Tania was wearing a Survivors' Network T-shirt under her coat. She was generous with her money, and she had paid to have them made for all of the board members. The coat check girl gasped when she saw it.

"You're a World Trade Center survivor? Oh! That's *so* cool!" she cried, gawking at Tania as if she had won an Olympic gold medal. "I wish I was."

Linda and Tania looked at each other in disbelief and then burst out laughing.

"Oh, believe me, you don't!" Tania replied.

To which Linda added, "Exactly! Are you out of your mind?"

Linda asked Tania to be her partner for the hunt, and Tania obliged. They spent the afternoon going through the museum, interpreting clues, bantering back and forth, and laughing until their sides ached. For the first time in as long as she could remember, Linda forgot about her pain and misery. For a few hours, she felt carefree, almost like a kid again. After 9/11, she felt like a rudderless boat adrift at sea. Now she felt moored to the other survivors. She had found a place to belong.

Linda was exhausted by the end of the day. All of the survivors were. It was late afternoon when they left the museum to go their separate ways. As everyone else scurried off, Tania and Linda lagged behind.

"I could go for a cup of coffee," Tania said. "How 'bout you?"

"Sure!" Linda replied. "Coffee sounds good."

And that night, both Tania and Linda knew they would be best friends.

DARKNESS ON THE EDGE OF TOWN

In the weeks leading up to the third anniversary, the survivors began to see a different side of Tania. She was sometimes sullen and unresponsive. Days would go by, and no one would hear from her, and she didn't respond to emails or phone calls.

What the survivors didn't know, but Tania confided to her new friend, Richard Williams, the survivor from the Oklahoma City bombing, was that she was suffering a crushing setback. "People ask me what's wrong, and I tell them nothing, because I just don't want to lay it on them," she wrote in correspondence to Williams. "In reality, everything is wrong."

Indeed, she was feeling so anxious and out of sorts, Tania said, that her therapist had encouraged her to take an antidepressant. She didn't know if it was the medication or recurring memories of the day of the attack, but she wasn't sleeping, and her mood swings seemed to be beyond her control. She said that some days she felt too depleted to leave her apartment. Other times she was unexplainably euphoric and felt like jumping out of her skin. She couldn't get relief no matter where she was. Being at Merrill Lynch's offices in the World Financial Center, overlooking ground zero, was a nightmare. She was always waiting for a plane to hit the building. And where once she had loved to travel, now she felt panicky every time she boarded a plane for a business trip, for fear that it would be hijacked and crash.

She didn't want to burden anyone, Tania said, but she really felt as though she couldn't go on. "It's like I'm damaged and will never get fixed," she wrote to Williams. "Frankly, I don't know how a bunch of pills is going to help me with my problems, but my therapist says that they'll take some of the emotional edge off so I can face my flashbacks and talk more about my experience."

Pills certainly wouldn't change the way the world continued to perceive the survivors, Tania complained. That was something she desperately wanted to effect. Why didn't people want to hear what she and the other survivors had to say? she wondered. Testimony from the survivors of Nazi concentration camps was painfully graphic, as it should have been. What was different about 9/11, when scores of innocent Americans were murdered in the name of a radical political ideology? Why were the people who bore witness to this holocaust expected to swallow their anguish and be as they were before the malevolent deeds of Islamic extremists intervened in their lives?

"It seems no one cares about how much I suffered, what I saw," Tania wrote. "How can that help people in the future? The rest of the world saw [the attack] from their TVs at home. They saw the towers burning and the people falling, but they didn't see what was going on inside. People need to know that the 78th floor was full of bodies, burnt and ripped apart, that were their fellow Americans, fathers, mothers, daughters, and sons. That cannot simply be hidden because it is too hard to tell or show. People just have to know about it because, just like knowing what happened in the concentration camps, only by understanding the true horrors of the day can we do something to prevent it from happening again."

Tania didn't want anyone to suffer as she did. It hadn't been very long ago that she was living her dream. Nothing was the same anymore. "Dave is gone, and I should have died with all those people on the 78th floor but didn't," she wrote Williams. "I lived, but so many things changed. Now I can't find meaning in anything I do . . . All of this makes me mad and makes me wonder what it is that I'm doing here. Why is it that I continue to be haunted by the images of that day? I'm so tired of trying to make sense of any of this, of trying to cope with my situation. I miss Dave more every day, and I just don't understand how it is that I'm supposed to do this without him. Just this week, I attempted to put away more of his things, but then I went and put them back. I guess I'm either not ready yet or it's terrifying."

As reticent as Tania had been at first to talk about Dave, now she peppered most of her conversations with mentions of him. Dave was one of those guys everybody loved, she told Linda. In so many ways, he was almost too good to be true. Of course, Dave had his quirks. He was always misplacing his keys and his wallet, he watched the movie *Braveheart* so many times that he could recite most of the lines, and he couldn't stand to be late, not even by a minute when they were supposed to be somewhere. That caused little arguments as she rushed to get ready, and he stood there, checking his watch. But those were small things. What she had loved most about Dave—what drew her to him right from the start—she said, was that he was never afraid to show his sensitive side. She had seen him leave his volunteer shift at the soup kitchen in tears because, he said, no one should ever be hungry. And being the hopeless and silly romantic that he was, he had unabashedly serenaded her with corny love songs in places like the subway or the middle of a crowded restaurant.

Dave was always thinking of everyone else, Tania said. She had always told him he was loyal to a fault, and she loved that about him. In high school, he'd been a championship wrestler, and, until his death, he regularly returned to his New Jersey alma mater to encourage the boys on the wrestling team, even if it meant foregoing other weekend plans. When he died, the team dedicated its season to his memory, and then the school held a beautiful ceremony at which they unveiled a plaque in his name to hang permanently in the lobby. She'd been so proud to be there with his family.

How would she ever find someone else after loving Dave? Tania would ask. He never missed a birthday, and, no matter where he was, he always made sure to call his family and friends to serenade them with the birthday song. He loved kids, and they'd wanted to have three or four. Their plans were eventually to move to the West Coast, and they'd saved a substantial amount of money toward buying a vineyard in California's Napa Valley, which they planned to name Esperanza, or "hope" in Spanish. They had a lifetime's worth of dreams, Tania said, but not enough time to make most of them come true. Suddenly there was no future. Dave was gone.

She was so grateful that they had gone ahead and bought a beach house in Amagansett in the Hamptons and had the whole summer there before he died. Dave loved the commotion of the city, but the ocean soothed him, and his favorite pastime when they were at the beach was walking the dunes in the morning as the sun rose on the horizon. During the summer months before September 11, they usually left the city by noon on Fridays, then fought the weekend traffic on the Long Island Expressway just to be able to make it to Nick and Toni's, their favorite East Hampton haunt, in time for dinner and the house special ricotta gnocchi. The house at the beach had so many reminders of Dave. His picture was in every room, and his softball uniform and Hawaiian shirts still hung in the bedroom closet. She felt closest to him when she was there.

Dave's parents loved visiting the beach house, Tania said, and they sometimes all spent long weekends there, usually reminiscing about him well into the night. His mother always claimed she could feel Dave in that house, and Tania felt envious because, try as she might, she wasn't able to "feel" his presence—only those two times: first, on 9/11, when she sensed him guiding her out of the World Trade Center; and again when she went to the footprints with the other survivors. She was grateful to have Dave's family still in her life, she said. Tania told a friend she'd met through her work with the survivors' group that she'd recently invited her in-laws to come to the beach for the third anniversary, and they'd eagerly accepted.

She'd initially promised the survivors that she would attend the ceremony with them at ground zero. It was to be their first time attending the memorial service as a group, and she wanted to lend them moral support. It was only after she'd told Dave's parents about her plans that things changed, Tania said. She had heard the disappointment in their voices when they realized that, for the first time since Dave's death, she wouldn't be spending the anniversary with them. She couldn't bear to let them down, so she'd changed her mind and invited them to Amagansett. It was probably for the best, she said. She had been feeling down in the dumps lately and wasn't sure how much help she would be to anyone else anyway. She hoped the survivors would understand. This was something she needed to do for herself and Dave's family.

The anniversary was only days away when Tania emailed the same friend to reiterate her plans for the anniversary.

She wrote:

I think I already told you that Dave's family doesn't want to go to the site this year. They get heartbroken with the way it looks. They don't like to see trains and construction trucks go by in their son's final resting place. Instead I proposed that we spend the day quietly in Amagansett, a coastal area in Long Island, where Dave and I bought a house. Dave used to love that place! We'll have a service there in the morning at a local church. Many friends are driving up there for the service as well. The priest is very nice and knows us well, so we asked him if it could be a mass and a memorial service at the same time, and he agreed. This means that we'll have friends and family come up and talk about Dave, and we'll also play his favorite songs. In the evening, we're going to have a sunset ceremony where we'll congregate at the beach, and we'll throw flowers and messages for Dave into the ocean. His old band will play, and we'll have a few beers and a BBQ, just as he liked it. We'll then get a fire going, and we'll talk about him all night till sunrise.

Dave's parents were private people who didn't fit into the very public 9/11 community, Tania told friends, so it was better that they spend the anniversary away from the probing eyes of the press. In fact, the only reason that she never revealed Dave's last name, except to her innermost circle of survivor friends, and only if they asked, was to protect his family's wish for privacy. If she had her way, she'd be spending the day at ground zero with the other survivors, listening for his name to be read from the roll of the dead.

On September 12 Tania was back in the city and more down-hearted than before. The time with Dave's family had only made things worse, she told the other survivors. Her father-in-law spent the afternoon on the jetty where Dave loved to fish, and she and Dave's mother shut themselves in the room where most of the mementos of Dave were kept, and watched, over and over, the video of the wedding ceremony in Hawaii. That had set the tone for the sunset service, she said, and she'd spent the entire evening consoling her distraught mother-in-law. More than ever, she needed to get away, and she planned to travel to her parents' vacation home on the California coast for an extended visit. Being with her family always seemed to help.

PART 4

2005

A TRIP TO SRI LANKA

Except for a few random emails, the survivors didn't hear from Tania for several weeks. Then, right after New Year's, she wrote that Merrill Lynch, together with other Fortune 500 companies, was deploying volunteers on a humanitarian mission to the countries in Southeast Asia that had been devastated by the Indian Ocean tsunami one week earlier. She had been asked to go and was one of the first to sign up. She and eight of her coworkers were leaving for southwest Thailand the following morning for ten days.

Tania told the group that she was keeping a diary of the trip and would share it with them when she returned. As promised, in mid-January she emailed a twenty-eight-page missive, single spaced, with exhaustive daily dispatches. In her first entry, on January 6, 2005, she talked about the long flight from New York to London and, finally, to Bangkok. The trip had been arduous, and the team was dragging by the time it landed in Thailand.

She wrote:

A colleague from our Bangkok office met us at the airport. He escorted us to the hotel and offered to entertain us for the rest of the day. After a shower and a change of clothes, this seemed like a good idea. It was better than sitting around waiting and thinking of the task ahead. He told us everyone remains shocked by the tragedy and that almost every Thai he knows has lost someone in the tsunami. This is starting to sound very familiar, and my stomach is churning already wondering how this trip is going to affect me. A dear Okie friend sent me an email on the eve of my trip cautioning me about the toll this trip could have on me, and I'm beginning to understand the wisdom in her caution.

After a delicious Thai meal, we visit Wat Arun, the Temple of Dawn, one of the city's most impressive temples. The sun is setting, and as the reds, pinks, and oranges inundate the sky, the temple shimmers, as its walls are made of pieces of colored glass. The beauty of it all contrasts with the reason why I'm here, and as I stand there taking it all in, I say a silent prayer for those affected by this terrible tragedy.

After walking around some of the city's most picturesque streets and doing some shopping, we head back to the hotel and say goodbye to our colleague. As we enter the hotel, we notice a large group of English speakers sitting at the lobby bar, and we decide to join in. Somehow a lonely hotel room doesn't seem appealing. As we mingle with the group, the topic of discussion becomes apparent immediately: the tsunami.

Some in the group are in the country looking for loved ones, others are members of the media who take breaks in Bangkok after days of reporting live from the different struck areas, and a few others are business travelers fascinated by being part of "it." We introduce ourselves, and suddenly we are the focus of the group. We get asked a lot of questions, and when their curiosity is satiated, they resume their conversations.

Tania went on to tell about meeting a couple from California who were searching for their missing daughter and her fiancé. She was particularly moved by their sad plight:

They have already been to Khao Lak, where she [their daughter] was vacationing in a beach bungalow. They looked for her, but their search turned up nothing. Both are listed as missing but not confirmed dead. They tell me about her and show me an album with pictures of them. She looks so pretty, so full of life.

I wish I could tell that mother how deeply I understand her pain, but this is a conversation I don't think she is ready for at the moment. I have exchanged contact info with her, and hopefully someday I can tell her. I know too well what it is to go through a loved one's effects to collect their DNA. I know too well what it is to apply for a death certificate without having the remains of your loved one. I know too well what it is to cling to the hope that they are not dead and then to finally have to accept the reality without being ready or equipped to do so. This is only the first day of this trip, and already all my old wounds have been opened. This was my reality not too long ago, and I'm reliving it tonight. I cry and cry for Dave, for myself, and for my family, knowing too well what I put them through. But as much as it hurts tonight, I think good will come out of this. In some sort of bizarre fashion, I feel this is healing for me even though I cannot feel it right now.

That was Tania, always looking for the break in the clouds. Two days later, she was traveling from village to village, helping to rebuild schools that were damaged and delivering supplies to people who had lost everything. "I have a very clear picture of what the tsunami must have been like and what the survivors have endured," she wrote. "It concerns me that while their physical wounds are being treated, their psychological ones are not. Having lived with PTSD for three and a half years, I recognize a lot of it: guilt for surviving while others died, intrusive thoughts, nightmares, the blank stare, etc. I wish more mental health professionals responded to a tragedy like this the same way rescue crews do. I wish I could do more, tell them it wasn't their fault that they couldn't hold the other person any longer, that they did enough by surviving, but I can see that a lot of their spirits are broken, and they will need a long time to heal from this. I think about how much my life has changed since 9/11. I remember when I volunteered with Habitat for Humanity through my company's social responsibility program, after Hurricane Mitch desolated parts of Central America in 1998. I spent a month building houses and schools, but somehow this trip means so much more this time around."

In yet another entry, she wrote, "Everyone here has a story, and it seems they are most eager to share them with one another. I sit there fascinated, hearing stories of rescue or survival, of friendship and bonding over hardship. I also share the reason why I'm here, and after the word spreads that I survived the WTC, I get introduced to a couple of people who responded to ground zero. Is the world small or what????"

She had learned so much about herself on this trip, Tania said. On the day before she was scheduled to return to New York, she wrote:

> For about a year now I have been debating what to do with myself. After all the pain I experienced, continuing working in the same place, doing the same things as my pre-9/11 life doesn't seem enough. I've been through too much. I've seen and experienced too much just to go back to my old life. I want to make a difference in the world, I want to help people, I want to work with children so that they don't hate enough to slam planes into buildings . . . I'm not sure of the long-term effects of this trip, but somehow it is transforming my memories of 9/11 and putting them in a less painful place.

When Tania arrived at the survivors' meeting later that month, everyone stood and applauded her. Her face turned crimson, and she giggled in that childlike way of hers. The others asked her to begin the meeting with a recap of her trip, and Tania obliged happily. For the next hour, she regaled the others with stories from those ten days away. The trip had done her good, she said. Tania had turned a corner in her own recovery while she was away.

Now she wanted to help them to turn a corner in theirs.

THE
SURVIVORS'
STAIRWAY

In one year, Gerry Bogacz's idea for a peer support group had grown into a budding movement of people searching for a purpose. Tania had taught by example. If you want to move forward, she told the others, get past yourself. Help someone else. Find a cause. "Live for something other than the pain," she said. Linda had heard Tania say that so many times that she'd adopted it as her own mantra. Tania didn't just talk the talk. That's one of the things the others admired about her. She lived the philosophy. There didn't seem to be anything she wouldn't do for the survivors or the network. She gave and gave of herself and asked nothing in return but a little appreciation and a commitment from the others that they follow her lead.

In her first few months with the network, she'd built the group a website, which she managed, and she'd organized a survivors' speaker's bureau. She'd facilitated a writer's workshop, met with publishers about producing a book of survivors' stories, and tossed around an idea for a survivors' documentary. In addition, Tania hosted fund-raisers at her tony midtown apartment to keep the network running, and she always contributed the food, the wine, and the use of the beautiful glassed-in party room on the roof of her building.

Her devotion to the group only intensified after her return from Thailand. After that, there wasn't a day that passed when Tania didn't propose some new initiative, some new way to ensure the network's relevance. Her mission was to get the survivors noticed, and she worked until her fingers blistered from punching the numbers on her phone and pounding the keys on her computer. She reached out to influential bureaucrats in the New York State Assembly and city hall, to the movers and shakers in the 9/11 stratospheres, and to survivors' groups from other disasters. Her emails to the other survivors arrived at all hours of the night, and they wondered when she ever slept. But it was largely due to these compulsive efforts that the survivors were gaining recognition and, at least to some degree, an identity within the cloistered 9/11 establishment.

Tania's energetic personality was the perfect complement to the more measured and cautious Bogacz. When he asked her to cochair the burgeoning network, because the job had become too much for one person—and because she was uniquely entitled, with her extraordinary story and with her impressively bold and unabashed pursuit of getting the survivors noticed—Tania hesitated at first. She was back at Merrill Lynch full-time, she said, keeping late hours and traveling the world for her company, and her survivor's story was no more significant or important than anyone else's. She worried that having the title might mean that the survivors had higher expectations of her, and she didn't want to shortchange them or disappoint anyone if her career took her away from the network, which was likely to happen now and again.

She certainly didn't need the recognition of a title to continue the work she was doing for them, Tania said, but if he really thought that giving her that official legitimacy would help push their agenda, and if no one objected to her having to be incommunicado from time to time, then of course she would consider his proposal.

In Tania, the group had found a tireless advocate and a passionate voice. Now the World Trade Center Survivors' Network needed a purpose—or, as Tania would say, something to dwell on other than themselves. The early part of 2005 saw the survivors gain inroads in many of the developing plans and policies for the rebuilding of the World Trade Center neighborhood. They had successfully lobbied for a say in decisions affecting historic preservation downtown, memorials to be built at ground zero, and the development of a tribute center at the site. "Things are starting to happen," Tania wrote Richard Williams in Oklahoma City. But as much as the survivors had accomplished in getting the recognition they deserved, she said, they still needed a project to call their own.

At the time, a controversy was brewing over a staircase that had provided the only route of escape for hundreds and perhaps thousands of survivors on the day of the attack. The thirty-seven steps that had once connected the plaza outside the towers to the street below had miraculously withstood the collapse of the buildings and the subsequent demolition of the ruins. The stairway stood, intact but alone, in the midst of the vast, empty landscape of ground zero—the last remaining aboveground relic of what had been the World Trade Center. Some people had dubbed the artifact "the stairway to nowhere." Both the Port Authority, which owned the World Trade Center site, and the Lower Manhattan Development Corporation (LMDC), the authority created in the aftermath of September 11 to lead the renewal efforts for ground zero, insisted that it had to go because it stood in the way of the rebuilding. Critics tossed in their two cents, some saying that the stairs were an insignificant eyesore and had no place in the blueprint for the redevelopment. But to many people, those craggy stairs represented much more than a bruised mound of chipped concrete and cracked granite. The staircase had been their passageway to survival.

Peter Miller, who survived both the 1993 and 2001 attacks on the World Trade Center, was a special projects manager for the Port Authority. His job was to oversee custody of the many pieces and artifacts left over from the attack. He was tasked with placing as many of the items as he could in museums and parks and other places around the country that would preserve and display them. He was also in charge of disposing of the items that his bosses determined weren't worth keeping. Miller mentioned to Tania that he'd been covertly working to try to save the staircase, but his job would be compromised if anyone from the Port Authority discovered what he was doing. The *New York Times* had made mention of the endangered staircase in a story about preservation efforts at ground zero, he said, but nothing had come of it. He worried that the powerful relic would disappear when no one was paying attention, and then it would be too late to try to save it.

If there was one thing Peter knew about Tania, it was that she could get things moving.

"What do you think?" he asked.

Tania was beside herself with excitement. What would be a more fitting mission for the survivors than to lead the crusade to save the stairs? It was exactly the project they needed to establish the WTCSN as a bona fide reform organization, and not just an encounter group. When she and Miller introduced the idea at the next Survivors' Network meeting, the others jumped on the concept of the campaign. Miller agreed to work behind the scenes, monitoring the Port Authority for information about its plans for the staircase, while Tania and the others began what was certain to be a long, uphill battle to save it.

In April, the network issued a press release to announce the initiative:

The World Trade Center Survivors' Network is launching the Save the Survivors' Stairway Campaign. This stairway is the only remnant of the World Trade Center complex remaining above-ground. It is located on the north side of the World Trade Center site near the intersection of Greenwich and Vesey Streets. While many have termed this remaining piece of stairwell the "Stairway to Nowhere," we prefer to think of it as the Stairway to Safety or the "Survivors' Stairway."

A widely circulated picture in the press after 9/11 shows people from Tower One who survived because they descended those stairs moments before their building collapsed. We believe that this was the only escape route for hundreds of survivors, after Tower Two collapsed.

The World Trade Center Survivors' Network proposes that those stairs should remain as a testament of hope to the thousands who survived that day. If restored and connected to a platform, the Survivors' Stairway could even provide a fitting vantage point from which survivors, and everyone whose life was profoundly changed that day, could gain a vantage point from which to contemplate the footprint voids, paying respect to their lost friends, colleagues, and loved ones.

Finally, we propose that development plans should be modified to dedicate a survivors' area on the plaza: an area where survivors could remember in peace and gain strength from the renewed World Trade Center community. The area should include the Survivors' Stairway. We hope that you agree that our stories are a poignant counterpoint to the tragic loss of life that day, and our proposal for the Survivors' Stairway creates a fitting prominence in contrast with the memorial design, Reflecting Absence.

The phone in the Survivors' Network office at September Space began ringing with calls of support for the initiative. Survivors who hadn't been part of the network volunteered to help. Other nonprofits pledged their support. Reporters called, promising to look into the plans for the stairs.

David Dunlap of the *New York Times* followed up with a poignant story about the plight of the stairs. Under the headline, "Survivors Begin Effort to Save Stairway That Was 9/11 'Path to Freedom,'" he wrote, "These were the final steps. After hundreds of workers made a terrifying floor-by-floor descent from their offices in the sky on 9/11, as the twin towers shuddered and rained ruin, they found a gangway to safety from the elevated plaza down the Vesey Street stairs . . . The World Trade Center Survivors' Network hopes the stairs can stay rooted. 'There's a great power in their being where they were,' said Gerry Bogacz, a founding member of the group. 'After the south tower collapsed, that was the only way anyone could get off the plaza.'"

The survivors had their platform. They had something to live for other than the pain. By committing their time and energy to saving the staircase, they were in essence saving themselves.

Tania was bursting with anticipation. She could hardly wait to figure out the next step in the campaign to save the stairs. "We've put ourselves on the map, and we have to make sure we stay there," she told Peter Miller.

"This is our time."

It was Tania's first brush with Dunlap and the *Times,* but it would not be her last.

TRIBUTE

At the same time the campaign to save the stairs heated up, the fledgling Tribute WTC Visitor Center issued an invitation for volunteers to lead walking tours at the World Trade Center site. As it was, every day, busloads of tourists from around the world descended on the spot to look through the slats of a fence into a naked hole.

Marian Fontana lost her firefighter husband there, and her advocacy work for grieving families mushroomed into the powerful September 11th Families' Association, the offices of which overlooked ground zero. She'd suggested the idea of the tours after watching Lee Ielpi, the father of another fallen firefighter, usher visitors on impromptu walks around the property. Ielpi, a retired New York City firefighter, had dug for two months in the infernal wreckage for the remains of his son, Jonathan, and he carried his body home in a basket when it was finally pulled from the ashes. It had been his idea to build an educational center where visitors would get a history lesson and hear stories such as his.

Fontana hired Ielpi and a civilian volunteer named Jennifer Adams, who delivered supplies to recovery workers in the aftermath of the attack, to make it happen. It was during those times when he was overseeing the progress of the Visitor Center that Ielpi corralled tourists and took them on tours. Fontana saw how much that effort meant to the sightseers, and how important it was for the proud father to tell the story of his heroic son. One day, after watching him speak to a group of visiting schoolchildren, she approached him with her idea.

"You know, I've been thinking," Fontana said. "Why don't we formalize what you're doing for tourists and train people to give tours?"

Ielpi didn't hesitate. "That's a great idea," he said.

In August 2005, with the opening of the Visitor Center still a year off, they had a syllabus and a tour route and were ready to train their first group of docents. An invitation circulated throughout the 9/11 community, calling for volunteers. The goal for the charter docent group was for ten people to be trained in time to give tours for the fourth anniversary commemoration the following month.

Tania was one of the first to respond.

"Put me in for the training," she emailed Rachael Grygorcewicz, a spirited young woman who had recently been hired as the coordinator of the volunteer program.

Being chosen for the guide program was seen as an honor, and many people who responded had to be turned away. The prerequisites for the position were nonnegotiable. Everyone who applied was required to fill out an application and be interviewed by the Visitor Center staff. The candidates had to be outgoing and personable and have solid public speaking skills and a memorable story that they were willing to share. Tania hardly needed vetting. By then she was the emblem of 9/11 survivors. Her inimitable story and upbeat personality took her to the top of the list, and the Visitor Center staff felt privileged to have the celebrity survivor on its docent team.

The inaugural training was set for a weekend in mid-August. The volunteers were asked to report to the Families' Association offices for a meet and greet and a screening of a film showing Ielpi hosting a tour for a group of primary school students. Afterward, the trainees were invited to a fashionable downtown restaurant to toast the program's official kickoff. Seated around a long table were Ielpi and his staff and the volunteer guides. They came from every corner of the 9/11 community: a widow who'd lost her husband, three mothers who'd each lost a son, a couple who lived in a neighborhood high-rise and nearly lost their home, and Angelo Guglielmo, a filmmaker who had befriended Jennifer Adams when they both shuttled supplies to the disaster workers and who'd ended up making a documentary about the volunteer effort.

Gerry Bogacz sat at one end of the table, and Tania and Linda at the other. Angelo was instantly drawn to Tania. She exuded such goodness and warmth. All the volunteers wanted to meet her, and she graciously acknowledged all of them. She was in high spirits, merry even, giggling and engaging in the light dinner conversation and posing for pictures. After a spirited introduction to the program, Ielpi raised his glass, and everyone toasted the new chapter in 9/11 history.

The following morning, the docents returned downtown, ready to go to work. Tania arrived with Linda and Gerry Bogacz, looking fresh in casual slacks and a blouse. She stood beside Angelo, who was sipping a cup of coffee, and they struck up a conversation. Angelo was taken by Tania's bright smile. It was so genuine and contagious. She listened intently as he told her about his work at ground zero after 9/11 and his film about the volunteers. When he asked about her, she told him her story of survival and loss. By the time she finished, he was in tears. He just couldn't reconcile how the sweet, vulnerable woman standing next to him could have survived such an agonizing experience and still be willing to come back to the site to help others understand what had happened there. With the training about to start, the two embraced and exchanged email addresses. They promised to get together again, and Angelo knew that Tania was someone he wanted to get to know better.

Over the next eight hours, the tour guides became experts on the history of the World Trade Center and both the 1993 and 2001 attacks. The idea was that they would follow a script with historical and factual details about the attacks, and then weave in their own personal stories. At the end of the day, they were escorted outside to conduct practice tours along the perimeter of ground zero. The exercise brought up different feelings for each of them. Linda had to fight off her unresolved feelings of illegitimacy, because she had neither lost a loved one nor been inside the towers. Bogacz struggled with feeling that the tours were part of his penance for surviving, as well as how much of his personal story he was comfortable sharing with strangers. But Tania? A natural. She sailed through her practice tour as if she'd performed it a thousand times. Everyone had stories, but not like hers, and her telling of it was so detailed and evocative that the others were all captivated.

"My name is Tania, and I lost my fiancé in the north tower," she began. "I'm going to tell you about that."

Over the next hour, she was vintage Tania. One minute she was making everyone cry, and the next minute she was cracking jokes and putting them all in stitches. Ielpi was in awe of her performance.

He knew he had a star.

BEST FRIENDS FOREVER

Tania and Linda's friendship had developed rapidly after the museum scavenger hunt. They never missed a day without at least talking on the phone. Some nights Linda left her job as an administrative assistant with a brokerage firm on Wall Street and took the subway to midtown to spend time with Tania before going home. The two would have dinner at a neighborhood restaurant or order in Thai, and talk until Linda had to leave to catch the last train back to Hoboken. When they weren't discussing something involving the Survivors' Network, their conversations were usually typical girl-friend chatter: Linda talking about dieting or her experiences meeting men through an online dating service, which made Tania howl with laughter. They even had nicknames for each other: Tania was T-Bone; Linda was Blondie.

Tania was different from anyone Linda had ever known. It wasn't just that she was so much fun to be around or that she had conquered such adversity. Tania was Linda's sign that God had been present on September 11, and she needed to hold onto that. When Linda was with Tania, she felt invincible. She was certain that they could walk together down Broadway, and if she jumped in front of a speeding cab, she'd be spared. The only explanation for Tania's miraculous survival on 9/11 was that she was protected by a higher power. Sometimes Linda would touch her friend's hair and think, "God touched this." God or a guardian angel, whatever it was, Tania was in divine hands. So as long as she was with Tania, Linda was covered. Nothing bad was going to happen.

At the same time that Tania's relationship with Linda was coming into full bloom, she was growing closer to two other women from the network.

Elia Zedeño was a financial analyst for the Port Authority. A small but robust woman with short, curly black hair and cheeks that billowed when she laughed, she lived in Jersey City with her sister and their adopted son. Elia, as contemplative as she was compassionate, was always looking for the bigger meaning of things. Her life had been a series of adversities that she had proudly overcome. She was just an adolescent when her parents left Cuba for America, but she had managed to balance both cultures in a very short time. Two years out of high school, she'd landed a clerical job at the Port Authority offices in the north tower of the World Trade Center, and she'd gradually worked her way up to a management position and an office on the seventy-third floor.

The first time the terrorists struck, in 1993, she had been riding an express elevator with five other people, including an intern she'd been showing around the towers. The pair had grabbed a snack at the food court and were headed back up to the Port Authority's offices when the bomb exploded in the basement of the north tower, sending shock waves through the lower floors. The elevator rattled, then plunged a few feet and slammed to a stop. Smoke seeped through the cracks in the doors, and everyone began to panic. Two of the men she was trapped with had attempted futilely to yank the elevator doors apart. Zedeño managed to stay composed until the woman standing next to her dropped to her knees and began to pray the Rosary. That's when her whole body started to shake.

Things went from bad to worse when a man trapped in the next elevator banged on the walls and screamed that he was burning up. When he finally went quiet, Zedeño tried to prepare herself for the same terrible death. And then, as she turned her attention to her terrified intern, an inexplicable wave of calm washed over her, and she felt as if her soul had left her body and was hovering over the others. She was no longer a panicked passenger but an impassive observer. She wasn't sure how much time had passed when a firefighter finally came to their rescue, prying open the elevator doors and pulling everyone inside to safety.

When the building was repaired, she returned to work in the towers, wary at first, but comforted by the astronomical odds of such a thing happening twice. On the morning of September 11, she had just logged on to her computer and was checking emails when the airliner struck, eleven floors above hers. The building lurched, and she feared it was about to topple.

"What's happening?" she screamed.

A coworker shouted to her, "Get out of the building! Get out of the building!"

Zedeño grabbed her book and her purse but panicked and began walking in circles. Then she felt something—she would call it an intense energy deep within her—propel her forward toward the emergency stairs. She'd made it to the concourse just as the neighboring tower imploded. Scooping out handfuls of soot from her mouth, literally blinded by fear, she froze as the debris cloud rained down. A woman, someone she didn't know, took her by the hand and led her away. She surely would have died there on the concourse, buried beneath the tons of glass and corrugated steel that had once been a tower in the sky.

Elia and Tania had gradually gotten to know each other through their work on the Survivors' Network board. They had both joined at around the same time and were always the first to volunteer for the grunt work that no one else wanted to do. Like everyone else, Elia marveled at Tania's ability to soldier through her own terrible misfortune by working for the greater good of the other survivors. Elia took pride in her own resilience, but Tania—well, her fortitude was unmatched.

In Elia, Tania had found a strong advocate and a woman whose determination matched her own. In Janice Cilento, she found her "New York mom."

Janice was middle-aged and a new trauma therapist doing an internship for a program funded by Project Liberty, a social resources group founded for the victims of 9/11. She had come to the profession late, after recognizing how therapy had helped her own life. An Italian-American from Brooklyn, she smoked and she cursed, and she oozed compassion and concern. Her first assignment in the field was counseling victims of September 11—a tall order for the most experienced clinicians in her field but especially for a newcomer just out of school. She had begun attending survivors' meetings to offer her expertise and ended up part of the survivors' family.

September 11 threw a lot of things off kilter, and the role of the therapist in the complex aftermath of the attack was one of them. Especially in New York, where everyone was suffering from some form of post-9/11 trauma, it wasn't unusual for the distinction between professional and personal relationships to blur. Janice did her best to hold that line, but nonetheless she became a confidante to many in the network.

When she took a seat on the Survivors' Network board, she developed a relationship with Tania that was more familial than any of her other contacts within the 9/11 community. Janice admired Tania for being a strong young woman who was doing a hell of a job hiding her own pain by helping everyone else, and she was fiercely protective of her. Sometimes her devotion to Tania clouded her professional objectivity. In her eyes, Tania could do no wrong. Even when she did question her behavior: for instance, when Tania poked mean fun at someone or repeated a hurtful rumor, Janice excused it as a consequence of her trauma.

Janice wasn't Tania's therapist, but Tania's needs came before everyone else's in the network—and sometimes even before Janice's family. Every morning, the therapist sent her a text message letting her know that she was thinking of her, always signing it "Your New York mom." When Tania wanted to have dinner, Janice took a train into the city from Long Island to share a meal with her. When Tania phoned at three in the morning because she was having a bad night and couldn't sleep, Janice took her call and tried to calm her down. When one of Janice's survivor clients complained about a dustup she'd had with Tania, she took Tania's side.

Janice cared deeply for Tania. She recognized the void in her life with Dave gone and her parents so far away, and she was willing to fill the space. But there was more to the relationship than a loyal friendship. Tania, by virtue of her story, was a unique psychological study in trauma—a guinea pig, really—as the miracle survivor of an ordeal the likes of which few people had ever overcome. For Janice, an apprentice in the field of psychotherapy, studying Tania was better than any textbook could ever teach. If she could facilitate her friend's recovery, there wasn't anyone she couldn't help.

In return, Tania taught Janice lessons in humanity that were inspired. And inspiring.

THE INAUGURAL TOUR

Linda's answering machine crackled with Tania's voice. "Blondie! Call me as soon as you get this."

Another one of Tania's urgent phone messages. Linda had become accustomed to them. Sometimes it was just Tania being her normal impatient self. Other times she had something pressing that she needed to talk about. This was one of those times.

Linda returned Tania's call later that day. "What's up, T-Bone?"

Tania was breathless, frantic, and excited at the same time. She had gotten a call from Lee Ielpi of the Tribute WTC Visitor Center, she said. He told her that the inaugural walking tour of the World Trade Center site was scheduled to take place in less than a week, two days before the fourth anniversary commemorations. It was something of a historical event, with Governor George Pataki, Mayor Michael Bloomberg, and Ielpi's buddy, former mayor Rudy Giuliani, in attendance. Press from all over the world would be there.

"Oh my God! That's great."

Tania took a deep breath. Linda could hear her struggling to draw in air. Giggling and gasping at the same time, she said that Ielpi had asked if she would join him in giving the tour. He'd caught her off guard, and she'd said she would do it. Now she was having second thoughts. It wasn't that she didn't want to do the tour—or maybe it was, she wasn't sure—but she was panicking at the thought of it. She was seriously considering calling him back to say that she'd had a change of heart.

Linda bellowed into the phone, "Have you lost your mind? Of course you're going to do it, and you're going to be fabulous like you're fabulous at everything you do! This is such an honor, Tania. Think about what this will mean for the survivors. They could have picked a family member, but they picked one of us instead!"

Tania hemmed and hawed. She was comfortable with the idea of rubbing elbows with important people, she said. That wasn't a worry. Her father was a diplomat in Spain before he'd retired and moved with her mother to the United States, and she had grown up in prominent social circles. And, yes, if she did participate, the exposure for the survivors would be really significant; she knew that. Who could ever again question the legitimacy of the survivors' place in the 9/11 narrative, when one of them had taken three of the country's most powerful politicians on a historic tour of the spot where it happened?

"So what's the problem?" Linda squealed.

Tania's voice rattled with uncertainty. So much was at stake, and she wasn't sure she was ready, she said. She had told her story before, but only to small groups. This was going to be a mob scene, and she wasn't sure she could handle it. She didn't want to falter and fail Ielpi, or embarrass the other survivors, or herself, for that matter.

"What if something triggers me and I panic?" she asked pleadingly. "What if I forget what I'm supposed to say? And you know I don't trust reporters. I don't think I can do it."

Part of Linda's job as Tania's friend was talking her off the ledge when she was threatening to fall apart. She had done it before during other perceived crises. She certainly could understand the pressure Tania was feeling. The docent training had been only two weeks earlier, and they had practiced the tours for each other since then, but her first official tour would be seen by the whole world. Who wouldn't be anxious?

"Of course you're scared, honey, but everything is going to be fine," Linda said reassuringly. "You'll be absolutely great. They wouldn't have picked you if they didn't believe in you."

That was partially true. Tania had outperformed all of the other tour guides on her practice tour in August. She was spectacular; a natural-born storyteller. But the other reason she'd been chosen was that the Tribute Center folks needed funding and exposure. They needed to make a big impression with the tour, and Tania's incredible story stopped people in their tracks.

The days leading up to the tour were up and down. Tania was a wreck one minute, ebullient the next. She took the other survivors and everyone else in her path on the bumpy ride with her, calling and messaging at all hours of the day and night, sometimes looking for encouragement, other times begging for a way out.

"Are you sure I can do this?"

"Of course you can, Tania."

"What if I start to cry?"

"Everyone will understand."

"I'm so nervous."

"You're going to be great. You're a pro."

So it went right up until the day of the tour.

Tania arrived downtown that Friday morning dressed to the nines in a light blue linen skirt and matching suit jacket. A few of her fellow survivors were on hand to offer moral support. She had a severe case of the jitters. Her palms were clammy, and her upper lip glistened with beads of sweat. Linda and Janice promised to stay close to her. They'd be right there, they said. But Tania was overwrought. She was sorry that she'd ever agreed to give the tour, she said. And she still just might not go through with it. Couldn't someone take her place? she asked, wringing her hands and fighting back tears.

The people from the Tribute Center did everything to reassure Tania and try to assuage her fears. They brought her bottles of water. They rubbed her shoulders. They told her how brave she was to be doing what she was doing. How important it was. Lee Ielpi was positively doting, as tutelary as an overprotective father. There was nothing to fear, he said. She was among friends, and he wasn't going to let anything happen to her. He wouldn't leave her side, not even for a minute.

But what about the reporters? Tania asked. What if they began bombarding her with questions she didn't want to answer? To hell with the reporters, Ielpi said. They would have to go through him to get to her, and she didn't have to talk to anyone she didn't want to.

"Okay, kiddo?" he asked.

Tania, her mouth dry and her face flushed, promised to do her best. But Ielpi's Tribute Center colleague Jennifer Adams wasn't convinced that she was up to taking questions. At the last minute, she recruited their mutual friend Angelo to distract her and calm her down. The filmmaker was happy to oblige. He would do almost anything to protect Tania, after all she had endured. "Keep the press away from her," Adams instructed. "This is a big deal for her, and I'm worried."

The morning press conference to precede the tour was scheduled for ten o'clock in the former Liberty Deli at 120 Liberty Street, across from ground zero. Another casualty of the terrorist attack, it was to be rebuilt as the future home of the Tribute Visitor Center. But for now, the unfinished storefront consisted of nothing but studs, mortar, and bare wires. Reporters from all over the world arrived there with their pack mentality, jockeying for position both outside on the sidewalk and inside the building, pushing and shoving when they didn't get the spot they wanted.

While Linda and Janice watched from the front row, Tania and Angelo were tucked away on the far side of the storefront. Giuliani was the first to speak. On the morning of September 11, Mayor Giuliani and his entourage rushed downtown when he got the call that a plane had crashed into the World Trade Center. He'd been holed up in an office nearby, trying to reach Vice President Dick Cheney on the phone, when the first tower collapsed, and the avalanche of warped steel, crushed concrete, and shattered glass trapped him and his staff in the building. One of the most famous photographs from that day was of the mayor emerging from the cloud of cinders and smoke, his suit jacket dusted with grayish ash. His performance then and in the difficult months that followed had earned him the nickname "America's Mayor." Even after his term ended on January 1, 2002, Giuliani spent countless hours at ground zero, and he had an abiding affection for the 9/11 community.

"The Tribute Center is absolutely the appropriate way to deal with this site," he said, standing on a makeshift dais, as cameras clicked and reporters scribbled in their notepads. "It's at the core of what has to be done here. The future generations are going to judge us by how well we do this. Twenty and thirty and forty and fifty years from now, people are going to come back here because they're going to read about this in the history books and hear about it, and they'll want to see how we preserved it. If we do it right, then we will have paid part of our debt to the people that we lost here. If we do it wrong, shame on us. And this does it right . . . This is the spirit of September 11 being preserved forever and ever, and there can't be anything more important that we can do than do it right."

Tania shifted from one leg to the other, licking her lips and checking her watch. Angelo grabbed her hand and squeezed it. "Everything will be fine," he mouthed. She nodded tensely, her smile forced and tight.

A question-and-answer session was scheduled to follow Mayor Bloomberg's address, after which the tour would begin. "These tours will offer an honest and compelling understanding of what happened to our city and our country," the mayor said in his concluding remarks. "The volunteers leading these tours will give the experience of visiting ground zero the dignity and the respect that it deserves. That's something we owe not only to history but to the thousands of hard-working New Yorkers who gave their lives here . . . With the help of this new volunteer guide program, it's heartening to know that the story will be told with accuracy, with honesty, and with a great heart."

As the reporters started lobbing questions at the officials, a New York radio commentator leaned in and asked Angelo if he could snag an interview with Tania before the tour. Tania shook her head feverishly. "No!" she said, grabbing Angelo's arm. A Tribute Center staffer rushed to the rescue, pointing the two to a pizza place next door, the designated holding area for the dignitaries to wait for the tour to begin. No one would bother them there.

Taking a seat by the door, Tania and Angelo ordered two Diet Cokes and chatted about movies they liked and places they'd been—anything but what was ahead. Moments later, the politicians sauntered in and stood at the counter nearby. For the next few minutes, the three most powerful men in New York talked about their golf games, pretty women, and other guy stuff. Did one of them really razz Bloomberg about being short? Tania and Angelo sipped through straws, communicating with their eyes, stifling giggles, and trying not to let on that they were devouring every word. Angelo always knew how to make Tania laugh. For the first time that morning, she seemed to have forgotten her fears. And then Ielpi announced that the tour was about to begin. As the honored guests were ushered outside, Tania took a last sip of her soda and looked at Angelo, her eyes wide behind her trademark burgundy-framed glasses.

"Wish me luck!" she said, trying to sound cheery.

"You're going to be awesome, sweetheart," he said.

Tania stepped out of the pizza joint and into a media circus. Hungry journalists clamored for a picture and a few words with the inaugural tour guide. The most aggressive of them thrust cameras and microphones in her face and barked questions at her. "What floor were you on?" "Who were you working for?" "What did you see that day?" Angelo could see the fear in Tania's eyes. She looked so fragile. He wedged himself between the pack and her, and he swore he could feel her body quaking. He was about to shout at the crowd to move away, when, in the midst of the chaos, Tania pulled a cell phone from her handbag and began dialing. She was calling her mother in California, she told Angelo. Before he had a chance to suggest that she make the call after the tour, Tania was chattering in Spanish and waving him and everyone else away.

As it turned out, the call home seemed to renew Tania. Her mother must have said all the right things because when Ielpi waved to her, signaling that it was time for her to meet the honored guests and start the walking tour, she obediently joined him, looking confident and ready to go.

"This is Tania, and she is one of our guides," Ielpi said, placing a protective arm around her.

Tania nodded and smiled.

The governor and two mayors formed a semicircle around their hosts. Ielpi gave a brief overview of the abbreviated tour they were about to take—two short stops along Liberty Street and ending in a gated area at ground zero—and the group began walking. With the politicians flanking her, Tania led the way. She was talkative and animated. Janice and Linda watched with wonder. Tania had been a basket case. Now she was taking charge. The dignitaries listened attentively as she explained about the docent program. She explained how the guides had been trained well and were able to speak about not just 9/11 and the towers but also the attack on the Pentagon, the brave but failed attempt by passengers to commandeer United Airlines Flight 93—the plane that crashed in Shanksville, Pennsylvania—and the 1993 World Trade Center bombing. She was excited for the public tours to begin, she told the guests, and she had given several practice tours that had gone well. Her personal favorite tour stop was the Winter Garden Atrium. The ten-story glass atrium, which was connected to the World Trade Center by a pedestrian bridge and had shattered when the towers fell, was the first structure rebuilt after the attacks.

"There's one of the stops where I tell my story," she said, pointing toward the glittering glass dome. "When I look around, I see a lot of teary eyes."

Giuliani pursed his lips and nodded reverently.

Everything was going so well. Not only had Tania seemed to have conquered her nerves, but she seemed to revel in the attention from the officials. However, as the tour moved from Liberty Street and along ground zero, the path narrowed, and reporters pushed in from all sides, like cowboys herding cattle. Tania was trapped in the media crush. An NBC reporter stuck a microphone in her face, and she turned away. Her cheeks were crimson, and her eyes darted from side to side. Soon she was being swept along like a raft in the rapids. She forced herself to stifle a scream and warned the politicians to tread carefully. "Guys! Guys! Watch yourself!" she cried. Ielpi saw her struggling to break free from the mob.

"Walk quick, Tania!" he shouted. "Walk quick!"

Tania picked up her pace, staring down at the ground. She lifted her head for a moment and glanced around, as if she were searching for a way to escape. Her white blouse was soaked with moons of perspiration. By then the crowd had eaten up Linda, but Janice was still close enough to see what was happening. Janice shouted to Tania, but she couldn't hear over the din of the crowd. She was panicking. At one point, she attempted to walk away from the pack but was herded back by a member of the governor's security detail. She looked back and saw Angelo, but he couldn't break through the wall of people that separated them. All he could do was shrug. The tour stopped at the observation platform, and Janice managed to catch a glimpse of Tania. She was chalky white.

With the cameras pointed into ground zero and Ielpi talking more about what the public tours would be like, Tania attempted to catch her breath. No one seemed to notice that anything was amiss, only the people who knew her well. A breeze blew up from the basin and over the crowd, and she closed her eyes and turned her face to the sky. Why had she ever come here? she wondered. She had almost cancelled at the very last minute, and Janice had talked her out of it. If she was going to get through this, she had to get hold of herself. The sun warmed her face, and she took a few deep breaths.

Ielpi finished his talk and reached out to her.

"I don't know if you've had a chance to hear Tania's story," he said, "but she was a survivor of the south tower, up on the ninety-sixth floor. Tania? Please?"

Ielpi moved to the side, and Tania took center stage. No more than two feet separated her from the dignitaries, and their eyes were riveted on her. Maybe it was the encouraging words, or maybe it was that she knew the tour was nearly over, but with her back to ground zero, and the officials forming a human shield between her and the swarm of media, she described what happened to her on that awful day four years earlier. Speaking quickly but matter-of-factly, she hit on every heartbreaking aspect of her story, sparing no detail. She was back on her game.

"My story is I was on the ninety-sixth floor . . . We walked down to the sky lobby . . . I was with other people on the seventy-eighth floor, waiting for the elevators, when we realized another plane was coming . . . I was badly burned . . . Two angels took care of me that day . . . I didn't know who they were. My fiancé died in the north tower."

The politicians were mesmerized. Pataki, his mouth turned down in a frown, shook his head from side to side. Giuliani smiled paternally. Bloomberg's brow furrowed as he listened stoically.

Tania spoke for a while longer, as comfortable as if she were chatting with friends. "So that's it, that's my story," she said finally, standing on the precipice of that great chasm of grief, shrugging her shoulders and smiling like a little girl who had just performed in her first school play.

The reporters had strained in vain to hear what Tania was saying, but the politicians heard every devastating word.

Tania knew she was a hit. She stood there beaming. Janice, Linda, and Angelo were bursting with admiration. They were so proud to be Tania's friends. What a strong woman she was. Even during her worst moments, when she felt overwhelmed and the challenge seemed too great, she somehow always pulled it off.

The tour moved to the gated area above ground zero, where it ended. Pataki was the first to thank the guides. The tour had clearly moved him and the others. "We're very proud of you, and we're very grateful," he said, patting Tania's arm.

Giuliani leaned in and kissed her on the cheek. "Tania, you did a great job," he said. "God bless you."

"Thank you for coming," she said, shaking his hand and smiling demurely.

Ielpi looked on like a proud papa. Tania had been the perfect choice. It had been a shaky start, but she'd hit the ball out of the park.

The officials said their good-byes, and the crowd began dispersing. Tania asked Janice to stay with her behind the gate until all of the reporters were gone. Of course, replied Janice. As they watched the maze of press disappear, Tania broke down.

"Why do the reporters have to ask so many questions?" she asked, crying bitterly. "Why couldn't they just leave me alone?"

Janice was startled. Everything had turned out so well.

"Are you okay?" she asked.

She was sorry, Tania said. The tour had been exhausting, and she didn't want to have to face another reporter or answer any questions. If it hadn't been for all of those meddling journalists, she said, she might have actually enjoyed giving the tour.

"I don't know how much longer I can take this," Tania sobbed.

Janice patted her back and tried to comfort her. She said she understood Tania's frustration. She saw her being jostled and had tried in vain to get close enough to tell the reporters to give her space. But asking questions was the media's job, Janice said, and the only reason they pursued her was because her story was so important. Tania didn't care. She had talked to the people who mattered: Governor Pataki, Mayor Bloomberg, and former mayor Giuliani. She had done her job, and now she wanted to go home.

"You did great," Janice said.

"Really?"

"Really."

The women stood inside the gate to ground zero for what seemed like a long time, until they felt fairly certain that everyone was sure to be gone.

"What do you think?" Janice finally asked. "Is the coast clear yet?"

"Let's go," Tania said, stifling a yawn.

When they walked out of the gate, a very weary Tania found Lee Ielpi and Jennifer Adams waiting on the other side.

"Did I do good?" Tania asked.

"Very good," Ielpi said enthusiastically.

Tania's eyes lit up.

A few feet away, a Spanish reporter was waiting. He had asked the Tribute staff if he could have a few words with Tania, and they'd promised to try to accommodate him. Tania spoke Spanish, and courting the foreign press was important in promoting the Visitor Center in other countries, so that tourists from abroad knew to make a stop on their trips to New York City.

"It's up to you," Adams said.

Tania didn't answer at first. She stood there, biting her lip and twisting the top on her bottle of water. Janice knew that Tania didn't like disappointing people, and, after an uncomfortable silence, she decided to step in. If there was one thing about the survivors and their ranks that could be stated unequivocally, it was that they had one another's back.

That trauma-driven devotion was multiplied a thousandfold when it was Tania's back. She was, by dint of her place at the top of the hierarchy of suffering, their exalted leader. She didn't have to do anything that she didn't want to do.

"She's had enough," Janice said, making the decision for Tania and taking her arm.

"Maybe I'll do it later," Tania said sweetly, looking at Ielpi. "Is that okay?"

"Whatever you want is okay," he said reassuringly. "You don't want to talk, we don't talk."

"Are you sure it's okay?" Tania asked again, looking back as Janice led her away.

Janice and Tania breezed silently past the reporter. He watched with a puzzled look on his face as they disappeared.

Tania breathed a sigh of relief. But out on Liberty Street, one last TV crew was waiting. When they spotted the star survivor, they descended on her.

"What floor were you on?" the reporter barked, trying for a sound bite for the evening news.

Tania turned to Janice, who had been walking a couple of steps behind her. "Janice! Janice!" she cried, her arms flailing.

With the camera about to roll, Janice stepped between Tania and the news crew. "Can't you see she doesn't want to talk?" she snarled, her teeth clenched in anger. "When do you guys ever back off?"

She took Tania's hand, and they walked off, ducking into a nearby department store.

In a press release issued later that day, Tania was quoted along with the governor, the mayor, and the former mayor. "As a volunteer guide, I am honored to be able to help visitors understand my personal experience," she said. "By giving visitors an understanding of the courage and bravery of our loved ones, friends, and coworkers, we keep their memories alive and are inspired by their sacrifice. The Tribute Center gives a voice to our loss and reminds us that one of the most powerful things we can do to heal one another is to listen to each other's stories."

That night, she composed her own account of the day and sent it, along with a video snippet from the evening news, in a blanket email to everyone in the Survivors' Network. She was clearly exhilarated by the day. Under the subject line "Tribute Tour," Tania wrote:

Hehe. For those who missed it, here's a short clip about it. Notice the amount of cameras pointing at me. And notice who I'm giving the tour to: Pataki, Bloomberg, and Giuliani. Don't ask me what I said because I was *freaking out*! Oh my God! I was totally overwhelmed, and I had to tell my story.

It was a momentous day in the legacy of the survivors, and Tania was proud that she had pulled it off. Now if she could just get through the anniversary.

I WILL NEVER STOP CRYING FOR YOU

Two days after the tour, the survivors walked into ground zero under a see-through blue sky to join in the fourth anniversary commemoration. It was their first official time there as a group and yet another milestone in a hard-fought quest for acknowledgment. Tania had snagged the invitation, and the fact that she'd once again worked her magic for the sake of the survivors wasn't lost on anyone. She handpicked only the people with whom she was most comfortable to accompany her. Linda topped the guest list, followed by Janice, then Gerry Bogacz, Brendan Chellis, Elia Zedeño, Peter Miller, Manny Chea, and Angelo Guglielmo—and, at the last minute, Lori Mogol and Richard Zimbler, a couple who'd witnessed the attack from their apartment.

Tania had been uncharacteristically sullen and brusque before the service began. Over breakfast, she confided to Janice that she had considered skipping it to spend the day alone at the beach house in Amagansett. Anniversaries were hard for everyone, but for her they brought back not only the horrific memories of her life-and-death escape but also the void left in her life from losing Dave—a chasm so deep, she said, that it made ground zero look like a pothole. As hard as she had tried to make herself better, Tania confessed, she wasn't closer to feeling anywhere near the same kind of happiness she had known before her world blew up, and she didn't think she ever would.

As with the three previous anniversaries, thousands of people crowded into the World Trade Center site on that Sunday, September 11, 2005. Some of them carried photographs of lost loved ones, while others grasped tiny American flags, or single roses, or personal mementos. Tania, wearing a white survivor's ribbon on the left lapel of her navy jacket, clutched a handwritten letter to Dave and, in remembrance of how they met, a yellow toy taxi. Being at the site seemed to trigger her anger. As the roll call of the lost was read by brothers and sisters of the 2,749 people killed, and one woman wearing a bright pink blouse remembered, "My brother taught me to live in Technicolor," Tania pointed accusingly at the tour busses idling at the curb and the tourists clogging the sidewalk. They all wanted to be part of this hell, she said. They wanted to belong to it somehow. Everyone did. If they only knew that what they were wishing for was something worse than death.

Her mood only deteriorated as the morning progressed.

The crowd fell silent when the bell tolled at 8:46 a.m., the time that the first hijacked jetliner crashed into the north tower. Dave's tower. Tania stood a few feet from the others, dabbing at her eyes with a tissue and mouthing Dave's name. When Linda tried comforting her, she shook her head furiously from side to side. No! she barked. She didn't need coddling, especially not from someone who wasn't even in the towers that day and couldn't possibly understand what she was feeling. Linda had borne the brunt of Tania's bad moods before, but Tania had never assaulted her survivor status, and she recoiled with hurt feelings. The others felt for Linda, but they huddled around Tania nevertheless, offering comfort and support with their quiet presence. Whatever Tania needed, they were willing to give her, even if it meant just staying strong for her. After all, if the anniversary was difficult for them, for her it had to be hell, and they wanted to do whatever it took to get her through it.

The next bell rang at 9:03 a.m., the moment that the second airliner hit the south tower. Tania walked over to Angelo and grabbed his hand. He looked at her and saw that her eyes were squeezed shut, as if she were trying to extrude some terrible image. He was certain that she was reliving her memories of those excruciating moments in the sky lobby. Angelo held tightly to Tania's hand. She seemed to be in a trance, surely trying to fight off some horrific flashback. How much more could this poor woman take? he wondered. She had worked so hard to reclaim some normalcy in her life after 9/11, but the reminders were just too many and too terrible. He wondered if she would ever be free. The others looked on, feeling impotent and frustrated that there was nothing they could say or do to make Tania feel better. Silent moments passed.

The next voice streaming over the public address system was a familiar one. "Good morning," the speaker said. "I'm Condoleezza Rice. I am so deeply moved to hear the individual stories of brothers and sisters. To learn about the lives of those who died here. For we all know that no matter how many fall, each life tells a unique story, and that each death diminishes us all."

Secretary of State Rice commenced by reading a poem by the nineteenth-century English poet Christina Rossetti:

> For if the darkness and corruption leave
> A vestige of the thoughts that once I had,
> Better by far you should forget and smile
> Than that you should remember and be sad.

Tania's face flamed red with rage, and she burst into tears. She loathed the Bush White House and everyone in it. If it hadn't been for them, she always said, there wouldn't have been a terrorist attack. The towers would still be standing, and she wouldn't have ugly scars on her arm and her back, and she would still have Dave.

"What is *she* doing here?" she sobbed, as Rice's voice echoed through the open space. "Why does it have to be this way? Why did this have to happen?"

The others didn't know what to do. They had never seen Tania that agitated. Someone patted water from a bottle on her forehead. Someone else gently rubbed her back.

Janice and Elia stepped in and, speaking quietly and reassuringly, told Tania that it was almost time to walk down to bedrock, where she could pay her respects to Dave at the memorial reflecting pool. They would all go down with her, so there was no reason to worry. But if she wanted to, they could all leave, right then, in the middle of the service. No one would be upset. They just wanted what was best for her. No, Tania said. She didn't want to leave. She needed to have her moment at ground zero to honor Dave, to read her letter to him and to leave the toy taxi by the side of the memorial.

By the time it was the group's turn to journey down the long ramp to the footprint, Tania had regained her composure. The sun's rays flooded the towers' imprints, and the still water of the memorial shimmered like a crystal curtain. This was the place of the death of her dreams, and she walked haltingly toward it. Tania watched as others dropped colored roses into the reflecting pool and inscribed dedications on its wooden frame. A moment passed, and she pulled the letter from her pocket. The paper trembled in her hand. As the others looked on, she read aloud.

"Dear Dave. I will never stop crying for you. I can't breathe without you. Every single day I think of you. I love you."

When she finished, she tossed the letter into the water.

As the others walked back toward the ramp leading out of the hollow, Tania asked Angelo to stay behind with her. They were standing quietly a few feet from the pool, and she opened her purse and took out a photograph of a beautiful young couple in a tropical setting with turquoise water and palm trees.

"Look at this. This was us," Tania said, searching Angelo's eyes for a reaction.

The photograph showed a much thinner woman, looking lovingly at the handsome young man standing beside her. Angelo thought he understood the plight of the survivors, having seen the aftermath of the massacre with his own eyes, and maybe he did understand the others and what they were going through. But Tania's burden was so much more. She seemed to know his thoughts as he stood there, staring at the photograph, choking back tears while searching for the right words that just wouldn't come.

"Yes, that was me," Tania said finally, her voice faint and unsure, her eyes searching for acceptance.

"Look what this has done to me."

They held each other, and he wept with her.

At 12:36 p.m. the name of David ▬▬ ▬▬ was read. Linda and Elia looked at each other knowingly. Tania had told only the people closest to her Dave's last name. Now they looked around for her.

Tania was already gone.

A few weeks later, seemingly recovered from the trauma brought on by the anniversary, Tania remembered her husband in her own special way. In a letter to the survivors, she wrote:

> *Hi all,*
> *Today would have been my 4th wedding anniversary. I usually have a private ceremony, and it's a day that brings me closer to Dave. However, at a recent tour for the Tribute Center, I talked about how the WTC was a special place for me because Dave and I met there and got engaged at Windows on the World restaurant. I also mentioned that our wedding was going to be Oct. 12. Well, today I went to a focus group session for Tribute, and everyone there remembered and made it so special for me. I even had a card from someone from Tribute when I got home. It really touched my heart. One of the questions we were asked at the focus group was how the experience of being a Tribute docent has impacted our lives. We all said how much of a gift it was, and although it is hard at times, it really takes you a step forward in healing.*
> *Tania*

A STRANGER

For many survivors, the first step to deliverance from the mental maelstrom of 9/11 was still the online forum. It was certainly Jim Jenca's salvation. An ex-marine from Bucks County, Pennsylvania, Jenca was the married father of two, the kind of a guy with a hard-boiled exterior and a mushy heart. Fiercely loyal to his country, he had joined the marines in 1980, not long after a mob of Islamic students and militants swarmed the US Embassy in Tehran, Iran, taking fifty-two Americans hostage. He felt it was his patriotic duty. Jenca was completing his thirteenth year as a security manager for the Madison Avenue banking firm Credit Suisse First Boston when the towers were attacked.

His pager went off, and he had rushed to the site to help get his people out of the company's branch office there. He had headed down to the World Trade Center's underground command center but decided to turn back after discovering that he couldn't make telephone contact with anyone there. Jenca had just left the buildings when the first tower collapsed above him. As he ran for his life, he was knocked down and trampled by others fleeing from the buildings. Three strangers risked their lives by stopping to pick him up. But in his own haste to get away, Jenca ran past an elderly woman hobbling with a cane. He had never forgiven himself for not helping her. More than four years later, he was still questioning why he, a former leatherneck, hadn't had the guts to do for the old woman what the strangers did for him. The answer was that his inaction had nothing to do with courage. He was the victim of his own hardwired human survival instinct. Still, his survivor's guilt was eating him alive.

After September 11, Jenca changed from a fun-loving optimist who everyone wanted to be around into a brooding man with a short fuse and recurring thoughts of suicide. He had lost friends in the towers, and he was pretty sure that the woman with the cane hadn't made it out either. Rather than be grateful to be alive, he blamed himself for surviving. Jenca couldn't work, and he slogged through every day, mad at the world, alienating his family and friends. He sobbed at sad television commercials, and he snapped at his kids for every little thing. Inside, he felt utterly worthless. He knew he was in trouble, but he didn't dare admit it because marines don't fall apart.

It was only after he'd confessed to his wife on one particularly bad night that he felt everyone would be better off without him that he was forced to get help. Lisa Jenca was a nurse, and she and one of her hospital coworkers diagnosed him with post-traumatic stress disorder. He exhibited all of the classic symptoms. Jim did see a psychologist for a while after that. He pretended to be healing, but he continued to have dark thoughts. If that was what his life was going to be, he didn't want any part of it.

Then, late one night while his family was sleeping, he was searching the Internet for anything that could help him to understand what was happening and stumbled on the Survivors' Network forum. He joined that very night as one of the first members, and Tania welcomed him to the group. He truly believed that the camaraderie he found there saved his life. Like everyone else who met her, Tania inspired Jenca. That she had triumphed over such adversity meant it was possible that he could reclaim his life too. There were many times when he was feeling low that he would log onto the forum and gather strength from her posts. Especially in the beginning, Tania had gone out of her way to encourage him. Some days she spent hours talking him through an emotional collapse, and he had come to depend on her more than he did his own wife. When he finally met her, during the inaugural visit to ground zero, he felt as if he were in the presence of a saint.

The forum and the people who were part of it became as essential to Jenca's existence as the blood coursing through his veins. Every time he had a setback and thought about dying, he found someone there who understood the profound ache in his heart. It was that solidarity with the other survivors that got him through each day. But after nearly three years of pouring out his heart and developing the most intimate friendships of his life, things took a terrible turn.

It all started shortly after the fourth anniversary, when Jenca posted politically charged commentary in the forum. The survivors, of course, were of varying political stripes, and they tried to stay away from discussions about politics. Jenca was always being called out for his veiled pro-Bush, pro-war postings, but then all would be forgiven, and the discussions in the forum would go on as usual. That October, he posted a treatise that a friend with similar political leanings had passed along to him.

Under the subject line "Things that make you think a little," the piece was a long recitation on war and the military and read in part: "In the years since terrorists attacked us, President Bush has liberated two countries, crushed the Taliban, crippled al-Qaeda, put nuclear inspectors in Libya, Iran, and North Korea without firing a shot, and captured a terrorist who slaughtered 300,000 of his own people. The Democrats are complaining about how long the war is taking. But it took less time to take Iraq than it took Janet Reno to take the Branch Davidian compound." The last comment referred to the government's fifty day siege of the religious sect's complex near Waco, Texas, which resulted in the deaths of scores of followers and their children, and four FBI agents.

The second part of the discourse was of an exchange between Ohio senator John Glenn, a former marine pilot and astronaut, and his opponent Howard Metzenbaum during a 1974 Democratic primary. The story went that Metzenbaum, who had a business background, attempted to undermine Glenn's credentials during a debate by saying that he had "never worked for a living." Glenn volleyed back with a response that many believe won him the election. The senator challenged his opponent to go to a veteran's hospital and "look at those men with mangled bodies in the eyes and tell them they didn't hold a job."

Jenca prefaced the post with a note that said:

All,
I am sorry, but I feel I need to pass this on. I know this is politi-
cal in nature, however, it is fact. In my heart I know we, as Ameri-
cans, need to unite. I am prepared to take all of the penalty flags
that can be thrown by everyone.
Jim

Some of the other survivors raised objections to the political nature of the post, and Tania was beside herself when she read it. She
called Jenca and reminded him that she and she alone ran the forum
and that she had the power to accept or reject anyone who wanted to
use it. His posting was an egregious violation of the forum rules, she
said, and he was no longer welcome there. She was throwing him out.

Jenca was stunned. He fought back with evidence of past posts
from others that were of a political nature, including some from
Gerry Bogacz and one from Tania herself, just before the 2004 presi-
dential election, when she took an online poll of the survivors, asking
them to reveal what their votes would be. When Jenca said he was
backing Bush, she responded with a terse rebuke, saying that she was
disappointed in him and adding that he obviously wasn't as smart
as she had once thought he was. Her attitude toward him began to
change after that. She was dismissive and often ignored him when
both were on the forum.

Jenca didn't know it, but Tania had begun telling other survivors that she suspected he was a fraud; that he wasn't a survivor at
all and probably wasn't anywhere near the towers on that day. She
had made such accusations before, and those people had gone away.
One woman claimed that she was in her mail truck when the towers
crashed around her. Tania told everyone her story didn't add up. Another said she was near the Pentagon in a tour bus and had witnessed
the plane diving into the building. Tania questioned her story as well.

A third, Lisa Fenger, was in town for a meeting and witnessed the
disaster from a boardroom in an office building on Fiftieth Street

and Broadway. Fenger was so traumatized by what she saw that she ended up joining the network and made a point of attending survivors' functions whenever she was in the city for business. She walked the Tunnel to Towers 5K benefit run with Tania by her side. On that particular day, Tania was wearing a T-shirt with Dave's picture, which Lisa recognized as one of her colleagues from Deloitte. She had heard Tania talk about her husband Dave but never realized it was the Dave she'd known.

"I had no idea Dave and Dave ████ ███████ was the same guy," she wrote Tania in an email after the event. "Wow, the only person that my company lost turns out to be your husband. How bizarre." Tania never answered the email and never spoke about it. When Lisa mentioned the coincidence the next time she saw her, Tania retorted, "I can't talk about this. It's too painful. And I'm too fragile." Soon after that, Tania began a campaign to get rid of Lisa and told her she was no longer welcome in the group.

So when trouble began with the John Glenn posting, even though Jenca had been seen on film running from the towers, many of the survivors were already questioning whether he was, indeed, an impostor. Tania said she could spot a fake a mile away.

The emails between Tania and Jenca bounced back and forth as he attempted to defend his action, and she continued to refuse to restore his membership. "I feel you have abused your power as a moderator, and I will do my best to get back to the group," he wrote. "I feel that you have discriminated against me due to my political beliefs, and I will see if there is a course of action I can take. I feel that I belong there and am quite sad about this whole thing. You have just crushed my every inner self with what you did."

The more he pushed, the more Tania resisted, even when he appealed to her ego. "No matter what the end result, you will always be an awesome person in my mind," he wrote. "You were a true inspiration to me and still are. I have been so down at times with regard to 9/11, where I had thought that I could not go on and considered doing something very stupid. There were a couple of things that came to my mind and stopped me. They were my family and you. I know what you went through, and if you can go on, that gave me the strength to go on."

Tania wouldn't budge. She had removed him from the group, she said, because he had broken the rules. And the decision hadn't been hers alone. "I consulted with the others before I did it," she wrote. She wouldn't say who the others were.

Jenca emailed some of the other members he felt closest to, telling them that Tania had banned him from the group. "I am really devastated by this," he wrote one survivor. "I guess I am all alone, since no one will take my side." He was right about that. No one was going to go against Tania. Even the survivors who came to Jenca's defense tiptoed around her, suggesting to her that he needed the help and should be allowed back. Tania was unmoved. When she got wind of his complaints to the others, she refused to respond to any more of his communiqués.

After a week of watching his lifeline slip away and being ignored by Tania, Jenca saw her online and pleaded with her to be able to return to the group. In a series of instant messages, he reminded her about their heart-to-heart talks in the past and of all of the times he had said he respected and admired her. He meant that, he said. But he had never intended to offend her with his political posting or his emails telling the others about his expulsion. He had just needed some time to cool off to understand the error of his ways, he explained. Now he wanted to come back.

Tania's response was immediate but curt. She would reinstate him, she said, if he promised to respect the others and abide by the rules of the forum. "And an apology would help," she wrote.

Jenca said he was sorry and that he would do his best to follow the rules. "When do I get reinstated?" he asked. "When I cool off," she replied.

"Well, today is October 18. How long will it take?"

"Well, you've been bitching for a whole week. I can take that long too, right? . . . Now it's me that needs some time."

Jenca could hardly believe that the same sweet woman who had welcomed him to the forum almost three years earlier could be so callous now. She knew how fragile he'd been and still was. He had revealed to her his most intimate thoughts, even those about suicide at his lowest points. She knew that he believed he needed the group to survive, but she was playing a cat and mouse game about his coming back.

"Who is this woman?" he wondered. She wasn't the Tania he knew. She was a stranger.

Jenca checked his messages every day for permission to return to the forum. He could feel himself withering without his survivor friends.

Finally, he received an email saying he was back in.

It was signed, "Tania Head."

MEETING THE CROWTHERS

The voice on the other end of the phone babbled with excitement. Alison Crowther was at home in the New York City suburb of Upper Nyack. The caller was Kimberly Grieger, a friend from the Tribute Center.

"Alison," she said, "I think I met someone else Welles saved."

Alison's son, Welles, a twenty-four-year-old equities trader, was working on the one hundred fourth floor of the south tower when the plane flew into the building. He was a hero that day, and he had become a legend in death. Welles Remy Crowther, Nyack High School honors student, Boston College class of '99, volunteer firefighter, athlete, brother, son. For all that he had been in his tragically brief life, for the longest time he was known only as "the man with the red bandanna."

Welles was Alison and Jeff Crowther's only son. At first they knew very little about the day he died. Welles had gone to work that morning as usual. He called both of his parents to say the towers had been struck and that he was okay and on his way out of his building. He had made it down to the ground level of the south tower before it collapsed. His body was found six months later, along with the bodies of a group of New York City firefighters.

That was enough information to satisfy Jeff Crowther. But Alison needed to know more about their son's final moments. She wanted some sense of how Welles had died. Why he died. For months after the attack, she spent every day scanning newspaper articles and television shows for clues. In May 2002, buried in a *New York Times* story about the 102 minutes between the first plane hitting and the second tower falling, she found the lead that would give her answers:

A mysterious man appeared at one point, his mouth and nose covered with a red handkerchief. He was looking for a fire extinguisher. As Judy Wein recalls, he pointed to the stairs and made an announcement that saved lives: Anyone who can walk, get up and walk now. Anyone who can perhaps help others, find someone who needs help and then head down.

In groups of two and three, the survivors struggled to the stairs. A few minutes behind this group was Ling Young, who also survived the impact in the sky lobby. She, too, said she had been steered by the man in the red bandanna, hearing him call out, "This way to the stairs." He trailed her down the stairs. Ms. Young said she soon noticed that he was carrying a woman on his back. Once they reached clearer air, he put her down and went back up.

Alison gasped. That mystery man could only have been her Welles. He had carried a red bandanna in his pocket every day since he was eight years old. On the Sunday before the attack, he'd met his parents in Soho for dinner. He'd pulled out his wallet, and it was wrapped in the red bandanna. "Oh my God!" Alison cried. "It has to be him. I just know that was Welles."

Alison tracked down the women in the story and sent them a photograph of her son. Both said that, yes, he was the man wearing the red bandanna; the man who had given his life to save theirs and others. The Crowthers had since formed close ties with both Ling Young and Judy Wein.

Now, four years later, they were learning about a third person their son had saved.

The woman's name was Tania, Grieger said. She'd met her in the docent program and watched her give a tour. When she'd told her personal account, toward the end of her tour, she had said that a man wearing a red bandanna rescued her. He had snuffed out her burning clothing, led her down to safety, and then headed back upstairs to help more people. She called him her guardian angel.

"I'd like to meet her," Alison said.

Grieger promised to arrange a meeting. She called back a few days later to say that Tania had demurred because she'd had sticky experiences with family members of people who died in the towers. They always wanted to know too much about what she saw, and she didn't feel comfortable giving them those awful details.

Greiger tried again a few months later, and in February 2006 she called Alison to say that Tania had reconsidered. She would meet them provided that any such meeting would be completely private. The Crowthers were private people and rarely discussed September 11 with anyone but their very closest confidantes. Of course they would keep the meeting confidential, Alison promised. They weren't about to alert the media or anyone else. They simply wanted to know whatever she could tell them about their beloved son, Welles, on the last day of his life.

A date was chosen for later that month, and the Crowthers arranged for a private dining room at the Princeton Club on West Forty-Third Street in the city. Tania invited Janice along for support. Tania was petrified. On the cab ride over, she had worked herself into a panic. She wasn't going to say much during the dinner, she told Janice. She was just going to listen. Everyone knew that she didn't like talking with family members about her experience. It was too painful all around. They would have to respect her silence.

Janice did what she could to pacify Tania. "Their son saved your life," she said. "It's a gift that you can meet them and they can meet you. If my son had died, I would be thrilled to hear whatever you had to say."

The Crowthers were kind people. When Tania walked into the club, they embraced her as if she were a long-lost relative. She presented them with a box of expensive chocolates she'd picked up on the way. The candy in the box rattled along with her shaking hands. Alison felt for her. She certainly didn't want to do anything to add to this poor woman's burden. The private dining room was serene. For the first hour or so, the Crowthers took turns sharing stories about Welles. How he'd always doted on his sisters, Honor and Paige, and how, as a boy, he had loved fishing with his grandfather. They talked about their son's pride in playing varsity lacrosse in college and his dream of becoming a full-time firefighter. Alison tried to be stoic, but Jeff could barely get through a story without his lip quivering.

Tania listened quietly. The man who had saved her life sounded a lot like the man she married, she said.

"Now I'll tell you my story."

She started with getting to work on that morning and then quickly made her way to the seventy-eighth-floor sky lobby. That's where she encountered Welles. She had given up any hope of surviving when the stranger with the red kerchief over his mouth appeared, seemingly from out of nowhere. She heard him first, she said. He was shouting out general instructions, just as the *Times* had said in its story "102 Minutes." "To anyone who can hear me, anyone who can walk, I know the way out. If you can help someone else, help. There are people here you cannot help anymore, so don't try." When she saw him, finally, he was dressed only in pants and a T-shirt, but she wondered if he was a firefighter. First, he gingerly patted out the fire on her burning jacket, and then, as she cried out in pain, he explained that he was going to show her the way out. His voice was strong and self-assured, as soothing as the sound of ocean waves lapping on the sand. He had placed his hand gently on her arm and guided her to the exit. They started down, and he'd encouraged her with every step. She could make it, he said. If she kept her head and kept walking, soon she would be safe. They were a dozen or so flights down when the air cleared, and he took the bandanna away from his face. She had gotten a good look at him then. It was Welles. Definitely Welles. He promised she would be safe. The danger was behind her. She remembered that as he turned to go back up the stairs, he looked back at her, and she was struck by the kindness of his eyes.

"You'll be okay now," he said. "Just keep going down. I have to go back up and help other people."

Tania's telling of the story had been uncharacteristically brief;

more of a recitation than a recollection, but everyone was in tears by the time she finished. For Alison, who was a violinist, hearing about her son and his incredible courage was as beautiful as listening to Johann Sebastian Bach's Brandenburg Concertos played on a Stradivarius. She was spellbound and filled with deep emotion. Welles's last hour would be his legacy, she thought. Had it not been for her wonderful, brave boy, who knows how many others would have died?

The hour was late. As everyone stood to leave, they all embraced. Alison handed Tania a red bandanna. If it was possible that she could feel any closer to her son than she already had, she said, Tania had made it so. They promised to stay in touch. In fact, Alison said, every September they hosted a memorial concert for Welles. Judy Wein and Ling Young always attended. Perhaps this year Tania would come too? Tania said, yes, it would be an honor. The group began to part, and Tania hesitated, as if she were mulling over something. There was one more thing, she said after a moment. She had kept her burned jacket all these years because it was one of the last things that the man who saved her life touched and she couldn't bring herself to throw it away. They could have it if they wished, she said.

The Crowthers were touched by the gesture, but they said, no, they wanted to remember Welles in life. Besides, she had already given them the best gift of all. She had given them a last glorious glimpse of their hero son. For that, they said, they would be indebted to her for the rest of their lives.

The cab ride home was quiet. Tania dropped off Janice at Penn Station for the train back to Long Island before heading home. There was really nothing left to say.

As the cab pulled away from the curb, Janice looked through the glass at Tania. She had never seen her friend look so sad.

BETRAYAL

It was early that summer when Gerry Bogacz got the first inkling that things in the Survivors' Network were not as they seemed. He and Tania were manning a booth for the group at a New York City street fair. Gerry enjoyed Tania's company, and he had been looking forward to the day. In the heat of the morning, they'd guzzled bottles of water and greeted people and caught up, as friends do. But as the day wore on, and the crowd thinned, the conversation took a startling twist.

The two had been discussing future plans for the network, when Tania began talking about how dissatisfied the other board members were with the way things were going. Speaking bluntly, she said that they were questioning his performance as cochair. Everyone appreciated that he'd founded the group, but sometimes they felt as if they were stuck on a rudderless ship and drifting with no real direction. Bogacz was wordless as she ran down a laundry list of complaints. Some board members were disappointed that he wasn't pushing harder to save the Survivors' Stairway. Others thought that he hadn't been a strong enough voice as their representative on the 9/11 memorial committee. And he hadn't won many fans when he appealed to the board to open a dialogue with the local Muslim community, and chastised members for posting anti-Muslim rants on the forum. He should have known that it was still too early, and feelings were still too raw, to try to force that kind of amnesty. There were so many things to say, Tania said. He had his finger in too many pies, and he wasn't giving the network the attention it deserved. He delegated too much. He was too preoccupied. Too acquiescent. Too laid-back.

Of course, she had defended him on every point, because that's what cochairs did for each other. But as much as she cared for him personally, she said, she had to say that some of the criticism seemed fair. She was telling him these things only because she didn't want to see him blindsided. The job he did was fine for what the network started out as: a small peer support group. But now they had hundreds of members and lofty goals, and no one was confident that he could get them where they wanted to go.

Was it the message or the messenger that hurt him more? Bogacz wasn't sure. Tania basically said that the people he had come to care so deeply for were losing faith in him, that they no longer trusted in his leadership, and she'd said it with the indifference of a dissatisfied boss preparing to fire a negligent employee. He returned home that afternoon feeling as if he had lost his best friends, and he didn't know why. It had been he who, a year after the attack, suggested that something needed to be done to bring the survivors out of their shell-shocked cocoons. Having lived through both attacks on the towers and experiencing for himself the consequences of surviving such a catastrophic event, he had recognized that they needed one another if there was any hope of healing, and he had pulled the group together believing that survivors, and survivors alone, were one another's own best chance for recovery. The network had come a long way from those early days, and he had thought he was at least a part of that success. Obviously, he was the only one who did. Now he sat at his kitchen table wondering, "Where the hell did I go wrong?"

How do you act as though nothing has changed when everything you believed to be true apparently wasn't? Bogacz began to look at the other board members with a doubting eye. He had opened his soul to these people. He'd cried with them and divulged to them his most closeted thoughts and fears. Now he found himself questioning the loyalty even of those with whom he had been the closest. If they had been so disappointed with his leadership, or so angry at his political beliefs, why hadn't any of them said something before it became a them-versus-him fight?

Bogacz began to perceive certain slights from some members.

Decisions were being made without his input. Meetings were being held without his knowledge. In late July he was called to a special meeting of the board. It was a venting session, with Tania leading the discussion and the others confirming everything she had told him the month before. They issued him an ultimatum: lead, follow, or get out of the way.

Bogacz felt so betrayed. Getting up to leave, he said he was taking a leave of absence, and no one tried to dissuade him. He stayed away for the rest of that month and all of August, and, when he finally returned, he announced that he would remain on the board but was relinquishing his position as cochair. The board voted to eliminate the cochair position altogether, and Tania was elected president.

Whatever fears Bogacz had about being frozen out of the group were reinforced at the survivors' tree-planting ceremony on September 10, the day before the fifth anniversary commemoration. Two years earlier, the survivors of the Oklahoma City bombing presented the Survivors' Network with a cutting from their own Survivor Tree, an American elm that had been badly damaged but somehow survived the explosion outside the Murrah Federal Building. The sapling was kept in a New York City Parks Commission greenhouse for two years, and it had grown into a healthy six-foot-tall tree, ready for a home. Tania had arranged for it to be planted in the Living Memorial Grove, across the street from city hall, next to five trees from the World Trade Center Plaza. A hundred or so people attended the ceremony, and most of the WTCSN board was there: Richard Zimbler, Peter Miller, Elia Zedeño, Lori Mogol, and Linda and Janice, who were hovering around Tania. Both Tania and Linda attempted to get Bogacz to participate in the planting, but he stood far away from the others, feeling like an outcast. When some of the others wondered aloud why he wouldn't join them, Tania responded by grimacing. "Oh, poor Gerry," she said mockingly. "Look at him back there sulking."

The anniversary was different for the survivors that year. Five years had passed, and they were stronger and more alive. For the first time, they planned a schedule of events for the days leading up to the memorial service. There were panel discussions, concerts, and an art show, and, on the eve of the anniversary, Tania hosted a barbecue on her terrace. She had recruited Angelo to film the survivors at the ground zero ceremony, and he'd captured many of the most poignant moments of the service. In the hours of footage, all that is missing is Bogacz. For the first time, he'd chosen to spend the anniversary with his work colleagues. They didn't even go to the site but instead paid their respects from across the street in Zuccotti Park.

He kept a low profile after that, quietly going about his work on 9/11-related issues that were important to him. One of those projects was a long-term health care plan not just for survivors but also for all people who had been impacted by the attack. He had been working with World Cares Center, another 9/11 service organization, the executive director of which had had a series of contentious run-ins with Tania and other Survivors' Network board members. Tania blew a gasket when she heard. The board members issued an ultimatum to Bogacz: they didn't want any further association whatsoever with World Cares.

Bogacz, bristling, fired off an email to Tania saying that under her leadership, the group was becoming exactly what he hadn't wanted it to be when he started it. Survivors had their own unique problems. They were damaged and needed special handling. That had been the purpose of forming the network, to address those individual needs. Instead it was becoming a political machine with backbiting and personal agendas. How could they be so arrogant and dictatorial, telling members who they could and could not associate with, and even throwing people out based on dissenting opinions and unfounded suspicions?

"Why is it so difficult for [the board] to accept and incorporate differences of opinion?" he wrote. "Why is [the board] not opening meetings to all of the directors? When did we develop a cabal? When did we become so political that we stopped being a caring organization? . . . I am not in the mood to have [the network] become a purely political exercise. I am not in the mood to watch it dissolve into cliques. If it is to be that, good luck with it. I hope it doesn't come around to bite you like it did me."

Tania responded within minutes.

"Hey, Gerry," she wrote. "You know what, I think you're blowing this whole thing out of proportion. I haven't insulted you, I haven't been disrespectful, I haven't put a condition on your return. I love you as my friend and always will. I'm sorry you're getting stuck on something like this after all we've been through and with the potential we have to do great things."

The Survivors' Network board elections were scheduled to take place two weeks later, on October 25. The night before the vote, Tania telephoned Bogacz at home. She was calling him out of friendship, she said. There was no need for him to be at the meeting.

"Please don't come," she said.

"What are you trying to tell me?" he asked. "That I'm not going to be reelected?"

Later that night, Tania composed an email to board members Peter Miller and Richard Zimbler.

"Attached is the revised agenda and ballot," she wrote. "Peter, remember that mathematically you need to give everyone a vote except for Patrick and Gerry for a desired outcome." The message was clear. The makeup of the board hinged on Peter Miller's vote, and the "desired outcome" was that Gerry Bogacz disappear.

The meeting convened at six thirty in the organization's new meeting space at 22 Cortlandt Street. Bogacz ignored Tania's advice and arrived early. Everyone marked his or her ballots, and Tania and Linda counted each vote. Bogacz trembled as he waited for the outcome. These were the people with whom he had spent the last three years of his life. They had cared for one another and loved one another, and he needed them. He felt dizzy and sick to his stomach as he waited for the count to end. Finally, Tania read the names of the winners. He hadn't made the cut.

Embarrassed and ashamed, Bogacz left the building without a word. But outside, waiting for the bus home to the Bronx, he wiped away a torrent of tears. The rejection of these people, who had meant as much to him as family, felt like a slam to the gut. What had he done that was terrible enough for everyone to turn against him that way? One of the unspoken rules of survivorship was that you went out of your way never to hurt a fellow survivor. They were all in the throes of trauma. Their injuries were grave and deep, and you never knew what might trigger those festering wounds.

On the bus ride, he remembered other times, either when someone in the group hadn't been doing his or her share, or needed to be replaced on a committee, and Janice had always been dispatched to soften the blow. The campaign to expel him felt deliberate and mean-spirited. It hadn't been some inadvertent, ill-thought-out reaction to something he'd said or done. It had been calculated and ruthless. And Tania. He would have never thought her capable of such deceit. How could he have been so wrong? He cried all the way home.

Inside the Cortlandt meeting room, the mood was somber. How had it come to this? some of the board members wondered. What had begun as a philosophical disagreement over the mission of the network spun into an ugly battle of wills. At the same time, there was a sense of relief that Bogacz was gone. It was time to move forward.

THROUGH THE LENS

Filming for a survivors' documentary on Tania and the survivors began in earnest that fall. She had been after Angelo for months to do the project. At first he balked. He had already done a film about September 11, and he didn't think he had another one in him. The two had developed an intense bond since training together for the docent program. Their friendship was deep and comfortable. Tania seemed to appreciate that she didn't have to be a survivor when they were together. She got to be just Tania.

There were days that she would arrive at Angelo's Manhattan apartment and just lounge around with him and his partner, Gabriel. They took in movies and talked books. She had been their guest at the screening of Angelo's first feature documentary at the Tribeca Film Festival earlier that year. *The Heart of Steel* was a film about the civilians who volunteered at ground zero in the immediate aftermath of the terrorist attack, as he did, and she was moved by it. Soon after that, she'd begun pushing for a survivors' story. Throughout the spring and summer, Angelo stood his ground. He didn't want to do it. But Tania was as persistent as she was accustomed to getting her way, and, after the filmmaker viewed the footage from the fifth anniversary and saw how powerful it was, he finally gave in.

Once she got him to agree, though, Tania was almost impossible to pin down for an on-camera interview. She always had some excuse. "Why do you want to focus on me?" she would ask. "Why don't you film the other survivors?" For weeks, Angelo shot around her, filming the others telling their stories. He pursued her relentlessly, but she was an artful dodger. Even when he got her to agree to an interview, she always came up with a last-minute excuse about another pressing commitment and cancelled. Finally, he asked Linda to intervene on his behalf, and the filming was arranged.

Tania's first interview was shot in a church rectory downtown. She was a reluctant subject, but showing up was her mea culpa for having been so wily in the preceding days. She was remarkably composed as she talked about what her life was like and of moving forward. The past five years had been about working through her grief, she said. Over time, she said, "it had transformed into a drive. I was driven. For these five years, I've been working nonstop. I've been working at my job, I've been working at the Survivors' Network, for Dave's Foundation, for the widows' group. I turned it into action." The fifth anniversary had been a milestone in her healing. She was feeling better than she had since the attack, and she had been thinking a lot about moving to California to get far away from her memories of 9/11 and start over. "But I know I can never move away," she said.

The last interview took place on September 12 at Tania's apartment. She had ordered in donuts and coffee. She sat in front of the camera and talked about her Hawaiian wedding and how when she and Dave had gotten back to New York, a group of family and friends wearing Hawaiian shirts surprised them with a cake with an erupting volcano. They had never filed their marriage certificate because they were planning for the formal ceremony, and there hadn't seemed to be any rush. After Dave died, she said, a judge married them posthumously. "It was the saddest thing in the world, to become a widow, you know, like that," she said. "It's strange."

Tania was almost giddy when she talked about Dave. But when the subject changed to the day of the attack, her demeanor changed. She squirmed in her seat and groped for words. "The first thing I felt was the air sucked out of my lungs," she said. "I . . . I . . . I was flying through the air. I remember very well the pain of hitting the wall. I knew I . . . I was going to die, and I was just praying it wouldn't hurt. Then I passed out."

"What happened when you woke up?" Angelo asked gently.

"I wanted it to be a dream," she said, her voice helpless and childlike. "I wanted to find myself in my bed, but it wasn't like that. I was feeling a lot of pain. My brain didn't understand what was happening."

The smell in the sky lobby was overpowering, and she realized that her own skin was on fire, Tania said. "That's when my brain caught up with my body." She began stammering. She was reaching deep, pulling out memories so tender that Angelo felt almost guilty for bearing witness to her pain. He realized that she wasn't talking to the camera anymore. She was reliving the worst day of her life with a trusted friend. This was a Tania that few people ever saw. For the next few minutes, she spoke pensively about her experience. She told her story with a quiet kind of grace. Her humanity and courage almost brought him to tears.

"I just lied there," she said. "So many thoughts going through my brain . . . And I was thinking about all these things. My family and my friends and my life. And I think I wanted to die at that moment, and I really thought those were the last moments of my life. And I was very angry. I was very angry because I never thought it would end that way, and I was angry that it was going to end there and at that moment."

It was then that Welles Crowther appeared, she said quietly. "At some point, I heard him say, 'I found the exit. Anyone who can walk, please follow me.' I was scared; very, very scared. I could feel my heart pumping. I thought my chest was going to explode." She hesitated. "And . . . and . . . and I think the problem was . . . the problem was that I had looked around, and I saw my friends . . . my friends . . . my coworkers . . ." Tania shook her head and jumped out of her seat. "Oh, I can't do this!" she cried, running off camera.

Angelo comforted Tania, and she said she was sorry. There would be other opportunities for filming, but she was too overwrought to continue that day. He stayed until she recovered, then hugged her and went home.

That night, he lay on his bed and stared at the ceiling, wondering why God allowed good people to suffer.

IN MEMORIAM

The ride from Manhattan to Nyack was fraught with tension. Janice drove the car while Linda bore the brunt of Tania's anxiety. That usually meant taking Tania's jabs about her appearance or her intellect or anything else that was certain to sting. Their roles had become clear over the course of the friendship. Linda's job was to be loyal and deferential. Tania seemed well aware of Linda's dependence on the relationship, and she often exploited it by mocking or scolding her. Linda rarely pushed back. The suggestion that she wasn't quite good enough only drove her to try harder to please. The more devoted she was, the more Tania demanded.

For days, Tania had been working herself into a dither about speaking at Alison and Jeff Crowther's annual memorial concert for their son, Welles. She growled at Linda all the way there. She always said she loathed the spotlight and never sought it, that her role was to be quietly supportive of the other survivors. But the Crowthers had asked her to say a few words at the memorial, and she had no choice but to agree. How do you refuse the parents of the man who saved your life? She couldn't, and she'd painted herself into a corner.

Linda and Janice did what they always did when Tania was in a dither. They tried to get her mind off whatever was distressing her. Sometimes joking and cajoling worked for a little while. Now Tania seemed irritated by the banter. She stared at the speech in her hand and shook her head from side to side.

"I can't do it," she said. "You'll have to read the speech for me."

Tania went back and forth during the whole car ride. She couldn't do it. Yes, she would do it. No, she wouldn't; Linda could.

Linda tried to humor her. "No, Tania," she said. "You'll read it, and you'll be fine."

Days earlier, Tania had called Linda in a panic to say that she was sitting at her computer trying to compose her speech, and the words just wouldn't come. Linda had come to the rescue again. She took a train from Hoboken to Manhattan and went to Tania's apartment, where they sat down together and composed the speech. Now Tania wanted her to deliver it, too. The Concert for Remembrance was held at the Grace Episcopal Church in Nyack, a hauntingly beautiful old English Gothic structure made of stone and stained glass. The carved oak pews were full with hundreds of guests. Tania sat in the third row, flanked by Linda and Janice, just behind Ling Young and Judy Wein, the two other women who had stories of being saved by the young man wearing the red bandanna.

Before the musicians took their places, the Crowthers stood to dedicate a paschal candle sculpture of a phoenix rising from the ashes of the towers, which they'd commissioned as a tribute to their son.

"Our thoughts were how fitting to use the phoenix bird as a symbol," Jeff Crowther said, struggling for composure. "A symbol of rebirth. Rising from the ashes. Rising from a piece of steel that was once a part of the World Trade Center."

Tania fanned herself with the program and fidgeted in her seat. "I can't do it," she whispered to Linda. "*I can't.*"

As self-assured and composed as she usually was, she had suffered with stage fright all of her life, she told friends. Sometimes she was able to control it. Other times her dry mouth and shaking hands took control. She was a pro at giving presentations for work, but large crowds sent her into a tailspin.

Linda rubbed her back and reassured her. "Tania, you can do this," she said. "You must do this."

The first sonata tinkled sweetly, but neither the strum of a harp nor the airy warble of a flute calmed Tania. Her chest heaved with heavy breaths, and she fanned harder. Linda finally gave in. She couldn't stand to see her friend suffer so. She took Tania's speech from the pew and began to study it. Tania looked at her, her eyes popping with expectation. Linda simply nodded, and Tania sighed deeply. Everyone could see the relief on her face.

Ling Young was the first of the survivors to speak that afternoon. Her daughter had urged her to prepare something, she said, but she wanted to speak from the heart. Ling was one of the first people from the sky lobby that Welles had helped that day. She had suffered third-degree burns over 40 percent of her body and was lying in the sky lobby when he found her. He had shown her to the stairwell and then led her down to the sixty-first floor, where the lights were on and the air was clear, and she could proceed safely the rest of the way down without him. Her story was strikingly similar to Tania's.

"When my building was struck, I was on the seventy-eighth floor," she said, recalling that day. "There was no one alive except a couple of us. We didn't know where to go. You look around, and there's no place to go. So we just kind of decided to wait it out to be rescued. All of a sudden, out of nowhere, this young man with a T-shirt said, 'I found the stairs. Come with me.' And he said it with such strong command, I followed him."

She ended by thanking his parents for "raising a kid with such courage."

The air in the sanctuary was heavy with emotion. Tania's eyes filled up, and both Linda and Janice leaned in to comfort her. Tania had told Linda that she'd read about Young, and, since only a handful of people from the sky lobby had survived, she suspected they'd crossed paths that day, but they'd never formally met. Nor had she ever met Judy Wein, who had also been in the sky lobby. She had suffered a broken arm, cracked ribs, and a punctured lung and lost her boss, who was standing right next to her. Just like Tania's coworker, Christine. Still fragile from her experience, Wein had elected for her husband to speak for her, and his words were stirring.

"I was lucky to find my wife in a hospital that day," he said. "She had just come out of surgery, and she could hardly speak, but she wanted to tell me what happened. She told me she was in the sky lobby when the plane crashed into the building and everybody went flying. The walls came down, and bodies were torn into parts. Nobody knew what to do. Nobody knew where to go. Nobody was ready for what happened. Judy was watching, and waiting for the worst, when out of the darkness came a young man wearing a red bandanna. And he knew what to do. And he knew where to go. And he was ready."

And then it was Tania's turn. Jeff Crowther introduced her.

"Alison and I are really honored that we were able to meet, this past winter, a delightful person, a wonderful young woman, who was also trapped on the seventy-eighth-floor sky lobby in the south tower," he said, his voice cracking. "She was on that seventy-eighth-floor sky lobby, and she's here with us, thank God."

As the audience applauded, Linda and Tania walked to the altar. Tania stood off to the side with Jeff Crowther, who placed a hand protectively on her back, and Linda took her place at the lectern.

"Hi, I'm Linda and I'm going to ask Welles for some strength here because I'm going to be the one reading what Tania wrote, and it's an honor to be up here because I have an incredible friend now thanks to him," she said.

Then, reading from Tania's script, she delivered the most rousing address of the service:

When Alison and Jeff asked me to speak today, I sat down and stared at a blank screen, and I cried, unable to find the right words to say. What exactly do you say to the family of the man who saved your life and gave his in the process? But then I thought about what Welles would do if our roles were reversed and he was asked to do this for me. This is what gave me the strength to be here today.

On September 11, I was on the ninety-sixth floor of the south tower. I waited to get on an express elevator. As we waited, United Airlines 175 headed toward the south tower. The impact was brutal, and I found myself flying through the air, and I eventually crashed against a marble wall. When I came to, my back and my arm were on fire, and all I could do was hope it would be over very soon.

A young man named Welles had also survived the impact, and he took charge. He came to me and started patting my back. At first I was angry because he was hurting me, and then I understood he was actually helping me. In a very calm voice, he told me to stay awake. To me he was a stranger, but his calm made me calm. When I turned my head toward him, I saw a red scarf over his face. I did what he told me, and I stayed awake despite the pain, smoke, and the shock.

Months after September 11, my parents read the story in *USA Today* about a man who had saved many lives in the sky lobby of the south tower. They were immediately drawn to the story when they read this man wore a bandanna. Could this be the same man that helped their daughter? Even after five years, I still carry the burden of being alive when so many others lives were taken from us—including that of my husband, Dave. I am still here, and I'm trying to find a purpose for being here.

In my family, we have a tradition at Christmas. Each year we tell the children in our family stories drawn from our lives during the past year. The story they want to hear, year after year, is the story of the man with the red bandanna, whose courage stood taller than the twin towers themselves. I like to tell them that on the day the buildings burned down, Welles stood up to the heavens. By sharing it with them year after year, I know they will never forget it, and the message will carry on to their own children, the children of tomorrow, ensuring Welles's story will live on forever.

In many ways, I feel Welles and I keep each other alive. He took charge on September 11 and saved my life, and now I keep him alive with my memory of him. Welles, you are my hero. I live my life to make you proud.

THE BURNED JACKET

For months, Tania had promised to donate her burned and blood-ied Armani jacket to the new Tribute Center for a special exhibit of artifacts from September 11. The jacket was to be displayed in a custom-made glass case, between the torn and shredded turnout coat and helmet worn by Lee Ielpi's son when he was killed, and a window from one of the airliners that was found intact on the street after the crash.

Lynn Tierney, the president of the Tribute Center, and members of her staff had concerns about all of the donated relics. There was a fine line between respectful reality and what might trigger a family member or a survivor, or seem macabre to the viewing public, and the staff was profoundly mindful of that when it chose what would or would not be exhibited when the center opened that September. Many of those discussions centered on what effect seeing that jacket every time she led a tour would have on Tania. But she had insisted that she wanted the jacket displayed, along with the dead young fire-fighter's coat and the other mementos from that day. Not only could she handle it, she said, she was proud to have it there. But getting it was another story.

At first Tania said that the jacket was stored 120 miles away at her beach house near the end of Long Island, and that she would collect it the next time she was there. Weeks passed with no jacket, but no one from the Tribute Center pushed for it. Everyone was so fond of Tania, and nobody would do anything to upset her. Her ambivalence was understandable. She would get the jacket to them when she was ready. It was Tania who usually brought up the subject of the jacket. She had different excuses for not turning it over. She forgot it. It was still at the beach house, and she hadn't had a chance to get it yet. Her mother had it at her house in California.

Weeks turned to months, and the Tribute Center ribbon cutting was just around the corner. All of the exhibits were ready, but they still didn't have the jacket. Someone from Tierney's office called Tania and left a message.

Tania called Linda, who knew all about the jacket, as Tania had mentioned it a dozen times. It had been part of a blue Armani suit that she'd bought just before the attack, and it was stored in a garment bag in the house in the Hamptons, scorched and bloody. When she had mentioned wanting to donate it to the Tribute Center, Linda encouraged her. Now Tania was upset that she had ever offered to give it away. She couldn't bring herself to see it again. "I can't do it!" she cried. "It's too horrible. I can't go out there to get it. There's blood all over it. You have to call them, Linda. You have to go there and tell them."

Linda did as she was told, but she was upset with herself for doing yet another thing she didn't want to do. She went to the Tribute Center and broke the news that Tania wouldn't be donating the jacket after all. Tania wanted more than anything to continue her volunteer role as a docent and as a gallery guide, Linda said, and she feared that looking at the jacket in the exhibit hall every time she was there could set her back emotionally.

Everyone understood, of course, and the Tribute Center opened on September 6, 2006, without the jacket but with great fanfare. Angelo filmed Governor Pataki and Mayor Bloomberg helping to cut the ribbon. Tania stood in the background, quiet and smiling. After the perfunctory speeches, the event moved inside to the center's four galleries, where the visitors and reporters were led on a tour that took them from the building of the towers, through the day of the attack and its aftermath, to a pictorial commemoration of the dead.

The glass case that had been made for Tania's jacket held a cell phone used by Chuck Meara, who worked for the Port Authority, during his death-defying escape from the north tower. But a plaque engraved with a quote represented her story: "I made it from 96 to the 78th floor. Suddenly, I heard a sound like I was standing on a tarmac and hearing an engine. People started yelling, 'Another plane!' Then I felt the pressure, all of the air being sucked out of my lungs. Tania H."

EXPOSURE THERAPY

It was shortly after the Crowther memorial, during a docent tour at ground zero, that Sam Kedem met Tania. He had seen her on panels and at meetings for the Red Cross, the Tribute Center, and other 9/11-related organizations, and, of course, he had heard all about her, but they were never formally introduced.

Kedem was a trauma therapist who was in New York City on September 11 and got in on the ground floor of a free counseling program for people affected by the attack. He had planned to stay with it for a year and then return home to Miami to resume his career. But nearly six years later, he was still there, enmeshed in the floundering community. He had come in contact with hundreds of survivors during that time but had never met anyone like Tania.

The New York *Daily News* had gotten it right in a story it published on the official opening of the Tribute Center. Mike Daly, the tabloid's crusty columnist, was at ground zero when the towers collapsed. He noticed two of his friends' fire trucks parked nose to nose outside of the north tower, and, watching the building collapse, he knew he'd lost them. When he met Tania during a tour at ground zero, he was instantly taken with her.

"One way that Head has learned to cope with her own loss and horror is to tell her story to those who come to the Tribute Center, whose permanent exhibits opened with appropriate fanfare yesterday," he wrote. "She stood by the entrance with a beautiful smile that is her ultimate message to everyone these five years later. To behold Head's smile is to know the terrorists did not come even close to winning. To see that smile is also to be challenged to be as decent and positive as this true survivor." Tania really was an anomaly, and Kedem wanted to get to know her—perhaps glean something about the secret of her incredible resilience that could help his clients recover.

They hit it off right away as they walked from the Tribute Center to the World Financial Center and took a table at a small café in the indoor courtyard on that April day in 2007. Kedem was as easy to talk to as Tania was. He told her about his work, and she told him bits and pieces about herself. An hour or so passed, and he'd suggested they walk toward the river and talk. The courtyard had served as a temporary morgue in the days after the towers fell, and he felt uncomfortable being there. She seemed surprised by that. Walking along the Hudson, she told him about her constant struggle to close that terrible chapter in her life, and she admitted that her trauma symptoms were as frequent and as fierce as they had been right after the attack. She still wrangled with obsessive thoughts and survivor's guilt and flashbacks, she said, and her sleep was constantly interrupted by nightmares and intrusive memories. She had bought self-help books and DVDs and spent hours reading and watching experts rally on about remedies and treatments, but nothing had helped. As they prepared to part ways, Tania proposed an idea.

"I don't want to live in the pain anymore," she said. "I want to move past 9/11. And I want you to help me."

They began meeting once a week at Kedem's office on Eighth Avenue. By their third or fourth session, he realized that Tania's confident, happy exterior masked a deep and abiding sadness. She was suffering from as serious a case of post-traumatic stress as he had ever seen. The most mundane things triggered her. Just talking about a subway ride, or sleeping in the dark without a light, could bring on debilitating panic attacks in which she would become so hysterical and disoriented that they had to stop. Sometimes the hour was more conversational than remedial, and they talked about her travels around the world, or her lucrative career, and her connections to influential people in politics and the financial world. He'd learned a lot about her life that way. But even after their toughest encounters, she was able to pull herself together and go back to work. Sometimes he would offer to walk her the few blocks to the World Financial Center where Merrill Lynch had offices. The Craig MacPherson mural of Rio de Janeiro on the south wall of the lobby was a favorite of his, and he'd wait for her to pass through security, to the bank of elevators, leading to the office floors, then stand and study the piece for a few minutes before walking back to work. Treating the most famous survivor felt like a privilege. He was impressed with her political and economic stature, and he believed that the community needed someone like her: a stand-proud figure who was going forward and advocating for all of the other victims. He would do whatever he could to help her deal with her trauma.

Kedem was a practitioner of exposure therapies, where the idea is to repeatedly subject patients to anxiety-provoking situations or traumatic memories for as long as it takes for the brain to learn that any perceived danger is an abstraction and not real. Thomas Stampfl pioneered the controversial practice in the 1960s as a treatment for phobias. The psychologist found that patients who were barraged with details of the situations they feared eventually lost their fear. It was used frequently by the United States Department of Veterans Affairs to treat soldiers returning from combat, and, in some circles, was considered controversial and risky because a percentage of patients suffered setbacks from reliving the traumatic event. Tania was willing to give it a try.

On April 23, in an email to her friends Richard and Lynne Williams, apologizing for cancelling a trip at the last minute to see them in Oklahoma City, she wrote excitedly about her new therapist and his ideas for treatment.

"Last year I gave up on everything," she wrote. "I was so tired of the memories, the flashbacks, the grief, that I gave up. But now I found a new therapist that I like, and we just started working together."

Kedem was proposing a form of exposure therapy called flooding, Tania said. She would record her experience in the south tower on tape and listen to it every day. The goal was that she would eventually become desensitized to those debilitating memories.

She posted:

It's going to be hard, but I'm excited to finally be able to tell someone what happened to me that day. I've been carrying these memories with me for so long that I literally cannot live with them. This is probably going to be as hard as being there that day, and all of my awful memories and all of the guilt is going to come out. I'm scared at the prospect, but I'm also excited, and this is all I can think about. I feel like I'm bracing myself for this battle, one of the most important of my life, and that's all I have the energy for.

I don't even know if I will be able to do this, but I want to give it a try. When I'm not missing Dave, I have flashbacks, or nightmares, or a friend's baby reminds me of the life I lost. I can take it most of the time and pretend I'm OK, but other times, like this past week, it all becomes too much, and I need this so much because I don't know how much longer I can hold it together.

Tania had a habit of cancelling plans at the last minute. The Williamses had made several trips to New York to spend anniversaries with Tania, and she had promised to visit Oklahoma City several times but never made it. Once, she had invited the Williamses to vacation with her at her beachfront house in Amagansett, and then cancelled when they already had their plane tickets in hand. She was always apologetic and usually had a very good excuse, and her friends were always quick to forgive because, after all, look at all she had been through. Lynne Williams, whose own life had been torn apart after Richard's rescue from the rubble of the Murrah Federal Building, was even more understanding about the effects of trauma on survivors.

"My dear, dear friend," she responded. "You have no idea how much I hope that this therapy will be of help to you. As much as I would love to see you and share some hugs (some of that Okielove!), I'm glad you're not coming if it means you're making progress. We could see that activity was your defense against the pain—you weren't giving yourself time to feel it. Our simple lives didn't afford us a means of escape—mental or physical—after the bombing. That was the greatest blessing that we could ever have imagined. We met each memory, each obstacle, and each storm of dark emotion head on. It didn't come in tidal waves threatening to drown us; it came in like the tide, sometimes reaching way too far, sometimes at a safe distance. But we faced it every day, and now it's a tightly woven thread in the makeup of our lives. Richard and I have had each other to lean on. I don't know how I would have coped if I'd lost him. Your loss is so great that you'll never be the same person you once were. You still have so much love to give, and so much love being returned. Healing will follow. I will pray for your therapy, as I pray for you every day."

The first session took place in Kedem's office on Tuesday, May 1. With a tape recorder on the table beside her, Tania started at the beginning. *The subway ride to work with Dave that morning. The meeting in the conference room. People screaming. Counting down to Dave's floor in the north tower. The trip down the stairs to the sky lobby with her colleagues. Waiting for the elevator with her assistant Christine.* She seemed to be having an out-of-body experience. *The violent crash. Windows breaking. Walls crashing. People flying through the air.* She was sobbing and rocking back and forth in her chair. *Hitting the marble wall. Waking up on fire. Christine is gone.* "Oh my God! Oh my God!" *Climbing over body parts.* "Help me! Somebody please help me!"

Tania's memories were so raw and so real that Kedem's colleagues knocked on his office door to make sure that everything was okay. The tape ran for forty-five minutes. When it was over, she slumped in her chair, dazed and confused about what had just taken place. Kedem gave her some water, and she sipped it slowly. Her homework was to take the tape home and listen to it every night as many times as she could handle it until they met again.

Tania stood to leave. Her hair was damp and stuck to her head, and black mascara ran down her cheeks. Placing his hand on her shoulder, Kedem warned her that things would get worse before they got better.

CAPITOL HILL

We were very pleased to learn that the committee is looking into the growing problem of nonresponders falling victim to 9/11-related illnesses, because there has been a disparity to date between the resources devoted to rescue and recovery workers, as compared with the health and financial resources available to other groups . . . We recently polled over 1,000 of our members and found that for the overwhelming majority, their number one concern today is health issues affecting survivors. And health issues affecting nonrescue survivors are not limited to physical problems alone. A large majority is still suffering from various degrees of trauma.

Tania's trip to Washington, DC, to testify before a congressional committee was a coup d'état, and a milestone for the network that no one could have imagined when a small group of people began meeting in a church hall to cobble together a support group in 2003. The hearing of the US Senate Committee on Health, Education, Labor, and Pensions about the long-term health effects from September 11 was scheduled for the morning of March 21, 2007, in the Hart Senate Office Building on the Capitol Hill campus. The subcommittee was made up of a posse of political heavy hitters, chaired by Massachusetts senator Edward M. Kennedy, and including Hillary Rodham Clinton of New York, Orin Hatch of Utah, and Barack Obama of Illinois. Mayor Bloomberg led the list of presenters. Tania was to be the witness on behalf of survivors, and network board member Richard Zimbler helped her to prepare her statement.

"My name is Tania Head, and I am the president of the World Trade Center Survivors' Network," the speech began. "Our members are World Trade Center evacuees, workers from nearby buildings, Lower Manhattan residents, witnesses of the attacks, rescue and recovery workers, and volunteers."

The nine-page speech was a pointed and eloquent summarization of the hardships suffered by the segment of the 9/11 community that had been overlooked, and the first such manifesto on the survivors' behalf to drop into the laps of the US Congress.

Getting survivors funding for medical care was yet another of Tania's projects, and she was excited to have the chance to lobby the senators and their staffs on behalf of her group. She had even arranged to fly back early from a business trip to Savannah, Georgia, to be able to deliver the speech herself rather than ask someone else on the board to fill in for her. "Ms. Head goes to Washington," she joked to some of her friends.

Zimbler and the rest of the board had waited anxiously for Tania to return with a report. When no one had heard from her by that evening, Zimbler sent her an email.

"Hey, Tania. So how did it go today? I didn't see your name on the witness list on the committee's web page. Did you get a chance to network with Hillary or Obama's aides?"

At 10:57 p.m., Tania responded. She had just gotten home from the airport, she said, and she hadn't had a chance to report back before then because the day had been so full with meetings and networking and pushing the survivors' agenda. She hadn't gotten to testify, but her statement had been read into the record of the proceedings, she said. Reading her email, Zimbler could almost hear the excitement in her voice, and he was excited too:

> I did meet a lot of people, including Dr. Reibman, who heads the program at Bellevue. She has agreed to come and speak at one of our meetings and would like us to help her prepare a report about

long-term care and serve on an advisory committee that will advise the committee that works with city hall.

I got a lot of business cards and did network with Hillary's staff. I even reprimanded them because they still don't use the word *survivors* right. Much of what was said again focused only on rescue and recovery workers. Residents were mentioned, and I guess we are now referred to as "workers." Survivors of Sept. 11 are such second-class citizens that no one even mentions us.

Someone from Hillary's office suggested that we put out a press release this week thanking Sen. Clinton for her efforts and using the same text in our testimony to continue to draw attention to nonrescue survivors. I think this is a great idea, what do you think?

Mike B [Bloomberg] didn't mention survivors once, he just made an appeal to open up the 9/11 fund again so that rescue and recovery workers who are getting sick can be eligible to receive comp. Mostly so that the city is not stuck with the bill. Dr. Reibman was the only one who really spent a few minutes talking about nonrescue workers, explaining how many office workers/ residents are getting sick and how many more continue to show up. She said that unless they receive additional funding, at the rate they are getting new sign-ups, the program will run out of funding at the end of 2008. It's pretty depressing.

. . . I'm glad I went through it; it's a striking reality check. We need to do more to call attention to nonrescuers getting sick . . . Plus, it is really fascinating to see the wheels of government in motion. Hillary has a very commanding presence, and you can tell this is her thing. You know what, politics apart, when you see her in action, you can picture her as president.

. . . I brought a lot of copies of our document and handed over all the copies to everyone I talked to, including the media, so that's that. Sen. Clinton is interested in meeting with us, and apparently they thought the idea of inviting the committee to attend hearings in NY/NJ was brilliant. You would think they would think of these things.

Well, that's it for now.

Zimbler was proud of Tania. He had never seen anyone who worked so hard and was so committed. Just when he thought the Survivors' Network had reached its pinnacle, Tania moved it higher. With her as their leader, there was nothing they couldn't accomplish.

FLOODING

Linda stepped out of the taxi at West Fifty-Fifth Street and Tenth Avenue and looked skyward toward Tania's apartment. The living room lights were blazing in her friend's unit on the eighteenth floor of the luxury high-rise. Tania was waiting. "Shit." For three years, Linda had come to the now trendy Hell's Kitchen section of the city at least once a week before heading across the river to her home in Hoboken, New Jersey. That was their time just to be girlfriends, away from the stresses of the network. Most times, she and Tania would order in and spend the rest of the evening talking or watching movies. Linda always looked forward to the visits. But tonight she wanted to be anywhere but here.

Entering the building, she nodded at the doorman and walked through the modern lobby to the bank of elevators at the other end, her high heels clicking on the marble floor. She pushed the up button and waited. Her stomach was uneasy. No, that didn't begin to describe the way she felt. She was trying to fight back waves of nervous nausea. Why had she agreed to do this, damn it? Why was she always doing things she didn't want to do? Maybe she could fake the flu, or say that her mother needed her, or her dog was sick. Maybe she should just tell the truth: that she was scared to death of what was about to happen. The elevator doors slid open, and she stepped inside and pushed the button for Tania's floor. How easy would it be to just walk out of the elevator and go home? It really wasn't an option, though, not if she wanted to stay in Tania's good graces. Despite her furtive and hapless little wish that it wouldn't, the elevator glided upward.

Tania lived in apartment number 1803, a few doors down from

Andrew Stein, the former city council president. Every time Linda came here, she couldn't help but wonder what life would be like if money wasn't an issue. White-glove services, sweeping city views, and rents that had to start at $4,000 a month—she could imagine living in such luxury. The elevator stopped at eighteen, and Linda turned and walked haltingly down the sterile hallway toward Tania's apartment. Even before she could ring the buzzer, the door flew open. Tania stood in the doorway, smiling that Cheshire cat grin of hers. She looked good. Her hair was pushed off her face, and her dark jeans and short-sleeved shirt were crisply pressed, as always. Her brown eyes shone with excitement behind her dark-rimmed glasses.

"Hey, Blondie!" she said, motioning for Linda to come inside. "Are you ready?"

"Hardly," Linda thought to herself. For days, Linda had been listening to Tania talk about her new therapist and an intense form of treatment she was undergoing. It was all she had talked about lately, this flooding stuff. She had told Linda about the tape she'd made with Kedem and about her homework to listen to the recordings at home. She had tried a few times, she said, but it was too scary. The therapist suggested that she recruit someone she trusted to be with her during the exercise, and she had chosen—who else?—her very best friend.

Linda had put off this moment for as long as she could, and then she ran out of excuses. Fear hammered her now. She felt shaky. Nervously jingling the change in her pocket from the cab ride over, she hesitated in the doorway. She had been sober now for almost four years, and her resolve not to drink was strong, but as they said in Alcoholics Anonymous, "If you don't want to slip, don't go into slippery places." The floor beneath her felt slick. She tried stalling.

"Listen, Tania," she said, still jingling the coins, "I have an idea. Why don't we do this another night? I'm really not feeling up to this. Let's go out and grab some dinner at the restaurant down the street that you like so much. You can tell me all about your trip to Washington. What do you say? C'mon. I'll even treat this time."

Tania shook her head. Her eyes darkened, and her lip curled in disappointment. Or was it disdain? Linda recognized the look. That was Tania when she wasn't getting her way. She braced for the inevitable tongue-lashing.

"Don't be such a chicken," Tania said, mocking her. "You're scared! Ha! Why should *you* be scared? I'm the one who went through hell. All you have to do is listen to a tape with me."

Naturally, Tania was right. It was times like this that Linda didn't even feel worthy of calling herself a survivor. She hadn't been burned or nearly lost an arm, the way that Tania had. Nor had she lost a loved one in the attack. Who was she to refuse her friend who had endured so much and asked so little? Besides, she could never hear enough about what took place inside the towers. It was a morbid curiosity that her therapist said was a common symptom of survivor's guilt. If she listened to the tape, she would hear plenty of what went on, perhaps more than she had ever heard before. And, after all, she felt privileged, special, to be the one who Tania had picked to share such a crucial phase of her healing. How could she be so weak when Tania was so strong? Linda felt ashamed.

"I'm sorry, sweetie," she said, hugging Tania. "I don't know what's wrong with me. I'm such a wimp. I'd do anything for you. You know that. Please forgive me. Come on now, let's get started with your homework."

Linda heard the door lock behind her as she walked into Tania's apartment. It was a beautiful space, open and airy, with floor-to-ceiling windows and dramatic skyline views. Linda was always surprised by how barren it was. Some of the survivors believed the spartan décor was Tania's way of not committing fully to a new life. Tania jokingly referred to her furnishings as "shabby chic." The living room was bare except for a flat-screen TV, two beach chairs, and a couple of bookshelves, and the bedroom had air mattresses rather than a bed. The only item on the walls was a framed photograph of Welles Crowther, in the space where Tania had her desk and computer. Tania had plenty of belongings, she had told Linda: rooms full of furniture from the Upper East Side apartment, keepsakes from her extensive travels around the world, and albums filled with family pictures. But her past was stored at the house in Amagansett because she still couldn't bear to be surrounded by constant reminders of Dave.

While Tania boiled water for tea, Linda sat on a stool at the breakfast bar and made small talk. The night was clear, and Rockefeller Center twinkled in the distance. Linda saw the tape recorder on a lamp table a few feet away. A shiver ran through her, but she was determined not to let Tania see her squirm. She couldn't disappoint her friend by backing out, not again, now that they had come this close. The teapot whistled. Tania poured two cups of tea. Linda held hers to her lips. The warmth of the cup in her hands felt good, and swirls of steam moistened her face, soothing her for a moment. If only she could end the evening here, with the wonderful, warm tea and the good company of her best friend. That would be plenty for her.

Tania walked to the tape recorder.

"Ready?" she asked, her eyes wide.

"Ready," Linda said, putting her cup down on the counter and clasping her shaking hands in her lap.

Tania snapped on the recorder, and Linda sucked down a deep breath. The tape began with Tania talking about getting up on that morning with Dave in their Madison Avenue loft. It is sunny outside, but the loft is still chilly from the cold nighttime air. She starts the coffee, and Dave pulls out his favorite frying pan and cooks eggs, two sunny-side up for her, three over easy for him. They share sections of the newspaper as they wipe up the last of their eggs with slices of toast and gulp down the last sips of coffee. While she washes the breakfast dishes, he walks their golden retriever, Elvis. Dave returns, and they shower together, then dress and take the subway downtown to their World Trade Center offices, arriving at just after seven thirty. In a calm voice, Tania describes how, around an hour later, Dave calls her office to ask if she'll join him for coffee in the concourse. It has become a sort of ritual for them, sneaking in a few more minutes together before launching into the workday. But on this morning, she has an early meeting and can't make it, so they make plans for dinner, say their I-love-yous, and hang up.

Moments later, the first plane slashes through the north tower. She tries calling Dave but each time gets a fast busy signal and realizes the phones must be out. As she prays for Dave, she sees bodies falling from the north tower. The voice on the tape is quivering. People in the south tower are frightened and confused, Tania says. Should they remain in the building or go? The security staff announces that everyone should stay put; the south tower is secure and safer than the street. She tries to calm her staff, but people are frightened, so she orders them to follow her down the stairs to the seventy-eighth-floor sky lobby, where they can all catch an express elevator to the concourse.

Tania was staring straight ahead and rocking back and forth in her chair.

"Tania, honey, are you okay?" Linda asked. "Tania?"

Tania was in a trance. Linda braced herself. She had heard Tania's story before, but only in bits and pieces and never in so much detail. She wanted to stop the tape, both because she was afraid to hear any more, and primarily for Tania's sake. Yet she didn't dare take charge in that way. Wouldn't that defeat the purpose of the exercise? Tania wouldn't be pleased. The next sound on the recording is Tania sobbing; gut-wrenching sobs that go on for several minutes. Linda could hardly stand it. Her heart rate took off, and tears filled her eyes. She looked over at Tania, who was still rocking and now sweating profusely. She took Tania's hand. It was limp and soaking wet. She was relieved to hear next the soothing voice of the therapist: "It's okay, Tania. I'm right here with you. Take a breath, Tania. Take a deep breath."

After a short silence Tania is speaking again on the tape. Her voice is weak and small. "I'm afraid," she whimpers. "I'm so afraid." Tania says she sees a plane coming toward the windows in the sky lobby. A woman is screaming, "Another plane is coming! Another plane is coming!" Dozens of people are in the lobby, and no one seems to know what to do. The building jerks violently, and the sky lobby is bathed in a blinding white light as the silver wing of a plane slices through it. A rolling fireball is followed by a riotous shock wave. The scene in the sky lobby is surreal, and she can hardly grasp what is happening. Where is her assistant? Where is Dave? What will Elvis do without her? She can't die. She won't die. Not here. Not like this.

Now, while Linda looked on, Tania began sobbing inconsolably. Primal, guttural sobs racked her body. She climbed out of her chair. Hunched over, almost as if she were trying to climb back into herself, she began pacing around the apartment. Tears and sweat poured off her face, like water from a sponge. Her hair and her shirt were drenched. She seemed to have trouble breathing. Linda followed in her footsteps, terrified, trying to console her friend.

"Tania, can you hear me?" she asked. "Tania, are you all right? Tania?"

But it was as if Tania's consciousness had left her traumatized body. The tape continued to roll.

Tania is quiet for a moment but then lets out a visceral scream. She says she is looking at the lifeless body of her secretary, who is nearly decapitated. "She has no head!" she cries. "Oh my God! Oh my God! I'm going to die. It's dark! I can't breathe! My skin is burning! Oh my God. They're all dead. Everyone is dead!"

Tania was walking back and forth across the living room, dazed and gasping for breath. Linda felt so helpless, but her explicit instructions from Tania had been not to interrupt the exercise, no matter how desperate things got. Linda knew what was coming next on the tape. She didn't think she could stand to hear Tania speak of it again, but she had to be strong for her friend—that was her role. From the first time Tania had told her about the dying man with the wedding ring, Linda had not been able to get him out of her mind, as if she had been the one who'd encountered him in the sky lobby. There were nights she saw him in her dreams, smelled his burning hair, heard his pleading voice. She took a deep breath and waited.

Tania is describing climbing over burned bodies and severed body parts. Her voice is flat on this part of the recording. Perhaps she is in shock. Who wouldn't be? As she crawls over the snarl of slaughtered men and women, desperately searching for a way out, she notices a slight movement in the carnage. He is unrecognizable as a man. His face and body are charred black, and his skin is smoking. He has a few breaths left at most. She pauses, and he reaches for her. "Please," he says, his voice barely audible. "Please promise me you'll give this to my wife." With that, the man places his wedding ring in her good hand.

"I promise I will," she says.

She then tells how she stood up and could barely fight the assault of the searing fires and bitter smoke, when, just when it seemed impossible, she sees a man holding a red bandanna over his face. His commanding voice and penetrating eyes give her strength. "Please don't leave me," she says. With that, the tape snapped off.

Linda looked at Tania, who was now standing, slumped, still. She looked confused and bedraggled. Her neck was blotched with bright red hives. Her shoulders drooped with exhaustion, and large half-moons of sweat had bled under the arms of her blouse. "What happened?" she asked, bewildered.

Linda went to the kitchen and made Tania a cup of tea. They sat together in silence for what seemed like a long while. Finally, Linda tucked her friend into bed and prepared to catch the last train home to Hoboken. But before she could get away, Tania made one last request. She asked Linda to promise that they could listen to the tape again tomorrow. "Please, Linda," she said. "I need to do this."

"Of course," Linda said. "I'll be here right after work."

On the train ride home, Linda suffered the first panic attack she'd had in years. As the PATH train dipped into the dark tunnel running under the Hudson, and the lights of the city disappeared, she suddenly felt as if she were suffocating. That awful, familiar tingling crept up her torso and engulfed her head. Her vision blurred, and her breathing got shallower and shallower. She was overcome with terror and fought the urge to get up and run. Where was there to go? She was trapped, just the way those poor people who had hurled themselves from the top floors of the towers had been trapped.

"You all right, ma'am?" the conductor asked. Linda nodded, but the nod was a lie. Being Tania's friend was a hard job, and Linda was weary. Everything was always about Tania. What Tania wanted. What Tania needed. How Tania felt. For three years, she had catered to Tania's every whim. She had allowed Tania's cruelties to go un-checked and accepted her criticisms without pushing back. Because she didn't want to lose the friendship. How much longer could she devote that kind of time and energy to Tania, while disregarding her own needs? She needed to maintain her sobriety so that she could have the future she dreamed of, with a husband and children and all of those things that came with a healthy family life. How would she ever be able to move forward if she was constantly allowing Tania to pull her back to the past she wanted to forget? Linda tried to slow her breathing, to steady her hands, to blot out the ghastly images crossing her mind. The fifteen-minute ride was torture. When the train finally pulled into her station, she dragged herself the two blocks home.

That night, Linda dreamed of planes crashing into buildings and bodies falling out of the sky.

SHADOW OF DOUBT

For nearly five years, Brendan Chellis had listened to Tania's stories, and she, his. Brendan had been running late on the morning of September 11 and was walking through the revolving doors into the north tower, headed for his thirtieth-floor office at Empire Blue Cross Blue Shield, when the first plane hit. He froze as the blast blew down the elevator shafts, shooting balls of fire into the lobby, and he turned and ran just as it exploded.

As one of the original members of the inaugural online forum, Brendan had followed Tania to the Survivors' Network, and they'd spent plenty of time together. For a long time, he had noticed slight discrepancies in the things she told him. Little things, here and there, that seemed insignificant until you added them all up. Several times he held himself back from asking her, Which was it, had Dave been her fiancé or her husband? She had referred to him in both ways. Chellis always chalked up the inconsistencies to trauma or a misunderstanding on his part. But late one night in the spring of 2007, just as he was about to go to bed, something possessed him to search the name David ███████ ███████ online. He had scolded himself as he typed the name into the computer. It almost seemed like a breach of Tania's privacy.

Chellis didn't have any trouble finding out about David ████████. The man existed, all right, and he had died in the terrorist attack, just as Tania said. He had been a popular young man. There were websites and memorial forums dedicated to him, and he had been the subject of numerous newspaper stories in his hometown. Reporters and friends had mined his life story, and his biography was full of details from grammar school to his wish to attend Harvard for a master's degree. The sites and the stories covered the entire spectrum of Dave's celebrated life with one exception: there was no mention of a wife or a fiancée named Tania.

As taken aback as he was, Chellis could think of reasons that she might not have been mentioned. Maybe she had been on the outs with Dave's family? Or maybe Dave had been estranged from his family, and they didn't even know about her? Then he remembered her saying how Dave's mother had tried to take over their wedding plans. And she had talked about Dave's parents visiting Amagansett, and her long talks with his mother, and the foundation in his name that they formed jointly.

What was the name of that foundation anyway? Chellis scratched his head and tried to remember. Dave's Foundation? Dave's Kids? Dave's something. Nothing came up in his Internet search. He remembered that Tania said it was a place in New Jersey for underprivileged kids, and she'd offered to take the Okies there when they were in the city for the last anniversary, but he couldn't recall ever hearing anything about the visit. Maybe he would call Richard Williams and ask him about the charity. But he couldn't reveal his doubts about Tania. What if Williams didn't believe him? Chellis knew what happened to people who got on Tania's wrong side: they disappeared. He thought about Gerry Bogacz and Jim Jenca and all of the people who had left the network because she'd accused them of being impostors. Even more frightening than her wrath was other survivors' blind loyalty to her. Williams, Richard Zimbler, and Lori Mogol were among his closest friends, but he had no illusions about where their allegiances lay. Everyone worshipped Tania, and he couldn't risk losing his support network—the people who sustained him—because he had questioned her honesty.

Chellis decided to check newspaper archives for stories about Tania, to see if she had ever mentioned Dave's name during interviews. She certainly had talked to enough reporters in her tenure as head of the network, and, as it turned out, she had mentioned Dave, but never his last name. Hadn't anyone ever asked? he wondered. A snippet from the *Daily News* story about her docent work with the Tribute WTC Visitor Center caught his eye. The reporter had obviously known Tania's story when he took the tour. "Head had not told this group that her husband died in the other tower," he wrote. "She also did not say that as she crawled through the carnage on the 78th floor a man charred from head to toe placed a wedding band in her palm. She stuck it in her pocket and forgot about it until months later, when her mother went through the personal possessions the hospital had bagged." Could these have been oversights? Chellis asked himself. Or maybe she had just run out of time? Or maybe she hadn't mentioned those things because she knew there was a reporter there writing down what she said on her tours.

Chellis didn't sleep that night. He tossed and turned, wondering what to do. If he told anyone his concerns, he risked being banished from the group, and for what? For proving that she, for whatever reason, needed people to think she was engaged or married to Dave? To catch her in a bunch of white lies? If he were wrong, the very relationships that had brought him back to life after September 11 and sustained him to this very day would be gone.

He decided to keep his eyes open and his suspicions to himself.

SLAYING THE DRAGON

While Brendan was wrestling with his doubts about Tania, Linda grappled with how to tell her that she could no longer participate in the flooding exercises. The second session had been worse than the first for Linda. She was running out of excuses for postponing a next time, and each time she cancelled, Tania acted more annoyed. Linda didn't want to disappoint her friend, but she had gotten physically sick after the last time. Tania videotaped her reaction and then taunted her with it, calling her weak and pathetic, and threatening to share it with the others.

The whole thing was just too weird, too gruesome. Linda was overwhelmed by knowing that when she went back for another session, if she did, she would be forced to hear about the man, unrecognizable as a human being, and moments from death in the burning sky lobby, begging Tania to take his wedding ring and get it to his wife. She couldn't bear to hear the story again. She couldn't take watching Tania shake and sweat and scream, "Bodies are falling! Bodies are falling!" But she felt ashamed for copping out on her best friend, and she couldn't stand it when they were at odds with each other.

In late June, Linda called her therapist to explain what was happening. "You need to come in," the therapist said. Tania accompanied Linda to the appointment. That was Tania's idea; she hadn't been invited to go. She said she didn't want to be home alone that day and asked if she could tag along. She wanted to hear for herself what the therapist had to say. Linda wavered but finally gave in. But when they got to the appointment, the therapist made Tania wait outside in the lobby. Tania was none too happy about that.

"What's going on?" the therapist asked Linda after closing her office door.

The therapist knew all about Tania. Linda often spent half of each therapy session talking about how worried she was about her friend. Despite the therapist's attempts to guide the conversation back to her patient's troubles, Linda found ways to return to the topic of Tania.

"I'm having nightmares again, and flashbacks," Linda told the therapist, starting to sob. Wiping her eyes, she went on to describe the flooding exercises and her role to keep Tania safe while she was in a trance. It was brutal, watching her, Linda said, her hands shaking as she spoke. "I had always pictured what went on inside the towers, but I never knew until Tania relived her experience right in front of me," Linda cried. "She confirmed all of my worst fears. Now I can't focus. I'm having severe anxiety attacks. I don't want to be alone."

The therapist was furious at what she was hearing. Linda had no place playing the role of Tania's caretaker, she said, and Tania had no right to ask her to play such a role. She was Tania's friend. She wasn't her therapist, or her mother. Nor was she qualified to participate in such an intensive and grueling psychological exercise. Indeed, because Linda had suffered such a severe case of post-traumatic stress herself after September 11, she risked a catastrophic setback in her own continuing quest for normalcy.

"Why is she asking you to do this?" the therapist asked. "This is not something you should be doing. It's inappropriate for her to ask. You have to stop. All the work you've done, and you're right back where you were."

"But Tania will be angry," Linda said.

At that point, the thought of sitting through another flooding session was more debilitating than the fear of Tania's wrath. Linda hoped the therapist wouldn't back down. Her sanity was at stake, and maybe even her life. Who could relive the events of 9/11 every day and still live a happy, productive life? Linda had spent years learning how not to focus on the horrors of that day, and now that was all she could think about.

"No more," the therapist said, holding firm. "You can't do this anymore."

A sense of relief washed over Linda. The therapist had given her permission to say no. She had ordered her not to participate in any more of Tania's therapy exercises. When Tania heard what the therapist said, she would have to understand.

"What did she say?" Tania asked as they left the office and walked down Forty-Second Street toward the PATH train station.

"She said I can't do the flooding with you anymore," Linda said. "I can come to your place every day if I want to, but I can't help you with that."

Tania shook her head. "What's the big deal?" she scoffed, her tone biting and angry. "Why are you making such a big deal out of this?"

"I was traumatized all over again, Tania," Linda said, the strength of her therapist's words helping her to stand her ground. "I'm having nightmares. I'm always panicky. I need some space. The flooding. The constant phone calls from you. It's too much."

Tania stopped walking. Linda could see that she was beside herself with rage.

"You're so selfish," Tania said, speaking through gritted teeth. "All you ever think about is yourself. Do you know no one in the group likes you because of that? No one likes you, Linda. Everyone in the group talks about you behind your back."

Linda gasped. She was a perpetual people pleaser. No matter how much therapy she had, she'd never been able to overcome that. She'd do anything for anyone if it meant being accepted. Being liked. Tania hit her where it would hurt most. She had taken aim at Linda's delicate ego and swung as hard as she could, shattering Linda with her heartless words. Linda's throat stung, the way it does when you're choking back tears.

"I'm going home," she said.

Tania didn't respond. The look of disgust on her face said it all.

A MELTDOWN AT THE ST. REGIS

That summer of 2007, Tania had taken to disappearing for days and sometimes weeks at a time. She told her therapist that her flooding sessions were helping her to move on. Her progress was achieved no thanks to Linda, she said, whose own counselor had finally forbidden her to participate in any more of the flooding exercises because it had set back her own healing. After all she had done for Linda, the rejection was a real slap in the face.

After six years of feeling dead inside, Tania said, she thought it might be time to start thinking about what she wanted for herself and not doing for everyone else. She didn't want to be defined by September 11 for the rest of her life. It was in that light that she had begun thinking about keeping a lower profile within the Survivors' Network, she said, and maybe even divorcing herself from the group eventually.

That was all well and good, Kedem said, but between the widespread impact of her story, and all of the good she had done for the survivors, it was unlikely that she could live anonymously again. "You are the face of 9/11, and people will always know you as that," he said. Tania responded with a self-assured grin. "Well, believe it or not, I can change that," she said. It was a strange response, but the therapist didn't pursue it. In his mind, Tania could accomplish anything she wanted to, even if that meant becoming someone else.

At that point, though, she was survivor nobility. It was under her leadership that the survivors' group had gone from virtual obscurity to a formidable advocacy organization with power and respect. In its short existence, the network had recruited over a thousand members, forged important political alliances, saved the Survivors' Stairway from destruction, lobbied Washington for health services, and convinced the 9/11 Memorial Committee to give the survivors a presence in the museum planned for the World Trade Center site, ensuring that their legacy would be preserved for generations to come.

As if all of that hadn't been enough, next Tania spread her good will to the Tribute Center, where she had inspired hundreds of visitors with her story. So when David Dunlap of the *New York Times* was looking for a story to observe the sixth anniversary, Jennifer Adams didn't hesitate with a suggestion. Do a story on Tania Head, she said.

No news organization covered September 11, during or since, as comprehensively or as poignantly as the *Times* did. The newspaper had been awarded the 2002 Pulitzer Prize for Public Service for its sweeping coverage of the attack and its aftermath. Its "Portraits of Grief" series about the lives lost that day resonated with readers around the country and around the world, and the lengthy story titled "102 Minutes," which told in superlative detail what happened inside the towers from the first plane hitting to the second tower falling, evolved into a best-selling book. Dunlap's archive of stories related to the attack—including the one he'd written nearly two years earlier, launching the campaign to save the Survivors' Stairway—was vast. Other media outlets had run stories on Tania, but not the *Times*. Indeed, its reporting had been so absolute that Dunlap and his editors wondered how they could have missed her.

Tania told the Survivors' Network board that Adams had asked her to consider doing an interview with the *Times*. She remembered Dunlap's name from the story about the Survivors' Stairway. She said that, as she'd understood it, the piece he wanted to do for the anniversary would showcase all of the survivors. She knew a story in the *Times* would be good for the network. That kind of exposure would bring in more members and remind the public that the survivors were still around and struggling. The others urged Tania to sit for the interview, and she called Adams to say that the reporter could call her.

But as had happened so often before, almost as soon as she agreed, Tania began having second thoughts. She had never wanted her work for the Survivors' Network or the Tribute Center to be about her, she told her friends on the board. Frankly, the *Times* frightened her a little, she said, although she wasn't quite sure why. "What should I do?" she asked the others. But before Tania had a chance to decide, fate intervened.

One morning, as summer was winding down, Tania called Linda at work, and she could barely choke out her words. It had been weeks since their falling-out over the flooding, and they'd had no contact since. Linda had mixed feelings about that. Some days she relished the freedom that came with the loss of such a demanding friend. Other times she missed Tania so much that not being able to talk to her hurt physically.

"What's wrong?" Linda asked.

Tania said that her brother Jay had died after a long battle with cancer. She hadn't wanted to burden anyone with her family problems, but she couldn't deal with another death of a loved one, and she was coming undone.

"Please come, Linda!" she cried. "I need you."

Linda ran from her office and grabbed a taxi downtown. Tania's eyes were red and swollen when she answered her apartment door. She wanted to go to church, she said. Linda walked Tania to a nearby Catholic church, where the two sat together in a wooden pew and prayed the Rosary. From there, she took Tania to her apartment in Hoboken, and they sat around talking about Jay for the remainder of the day. Linda felt so guilty. How could she have abandoned Tania the way that she had? The poor woman had almost lost her life in the terrorist attack, and her husband was killed. Now she'd lost a brother too. How much could one person take? Linda wondered. "How can I help you?" she asked. "What can I do?"

"Just be my friend," Tania said through her tears.

"Of course, Tania. I'll always be here for you. No matter what."

Linda promised to hold down the fort while Tania attended the funeral, and she promptly sent off an email to everyone on the network's mailing list. Under the subject line "Very Sad News," she wrote: "I wanted to let everyone know that Tania Head's (chair/president of the WTC Survivors' Network) brother Jay lost his battle

235

to cancer last Wednesday. She is out in California with her family and I am sure would appreciate everyone's prayers for her and her family. Godspeed—we love you, Tania!"

Well wishes poured into the network. Tania's survivor friends took the news hard. They hadn't even known her brother was ill, and they couldn't fathom why such a beautiful person had to endure so much loss. When Tania got back to New York a week later, she told Linda that her whole family had gathered for the service, and everyone took turns telling stories about Jay. People had flown in from Spain and England to pay their respects. It was a touching tribute, and she was happy to have been there, but she was glad to be back home in New York, where she could lose herself in her work.

Tania quickly immersed herself in planning for the sixth anniversary, but her friends noticed something different about her. She was irritable and ornery almost all of the time, and she seemed to be trying to distance herself from the others. As always, Linda was on the receiving end of Tania's moods, and, as always, she tolerated the hurt that came with Tania's razor-sharp words. She worried that, between regurgitating September 11 during her therapy sessions, and now losing her brother, Tania was headed for a nervous breakdown.

In early September, her worry turned to panic.

Shortly after returning from California, Tania had told Linda that Merrill Lynch was arranging for her to meet with the families of eleven of her coworkers who'd died in the towers. Over the years, she had been besieged with requests to meet the families, and she'd always refused. She knew what they wanted—details about the last moments of their loved ones' lives—and she had always resolved that they didn't really want to know what she knew. Those images had nearly destroyed her life, and she still couldn't get through a night without closing her eyes and seeing a charred or broken body. How could sharing those terrible memories possibly help them? But for some reason—maybe it was having recently lost her brother—this year she had agreed.

Tania said that the meeting was scheduled for the first Saturday in September at the St. Regis Hotel on Park Avenue. Linda was worried about the effect it would have on her friend. "Call me if you need me," she said. "Call me if you need anything at all." At ten thirty that morning, Linda's phone rang. Tania was on the other end, sobbing. Coming to the St. Regis had been a mistake, she said. She had barely made it into the room at the hotel when the family members started bombarding her with questions. The atmosphere felt almost ghoulish, and she'd started to panic and look for the way out. When she wouldn't tell them what they wanted to know, they turned on her, yelling and screaming at her that she had no right to withhold what she knew.

"Linda, I need you!" she cried. "These people are so mean to me. They're screaming at me. I need you to come right now."

"Stay right where you are," Linda said. "I'm on my way."

Linda flew out of her apartment. She hailed a cab and went directly to the St. Regis, where she found Tania curled in a ball on the sidewalk outside the hotel.

"Oh my God!" she cried, leaping out of the taxi and running to her friend. "Tania! Tania?"

Tania didn't seem to hear. She rocked back and forth, crying and shaking. "I tried to get them out," she wailed. "I tried to save them. I tried. Really I did. I didn't want them to die."

Linda was terrified. Tania was having flashbacks, just as she had during the flooding exercises. Linda pulled a wad of tissues from her purse and mopped Tania's forehead. She needed to get her inside, to get help. She took Tania's arm and gently coaxed her to her feet. Guiding her into the hotel lobby, she put her in a chair and marched to the front desk, demanding to know where the Merrill Lynch meeting was taking place. She was going to give those people a piece of her mind. How dare they treat her friend like that? Didn't they understand what she had been through?

The desk clerk looked baffled. "I don't know what you're talking about," he said. Before she had time to think of a retort, Linda saw Tania beckoning her. The poor woman looked desperate. Linda threw up her hands and went to her. "It's going to be okay, Tania," she said, speaking quietly and reassuringly. "No one can hurt you now. I'm here with you."

"I want to go to Dave," Tania said, her voice thin and wobbly.

Linda knew what that meant. During Tania's lowest moments, she often visited the Marsh & McLennan Memorial Wall outside the company headquarters in midtown. The glass wall was etched with the names of the 295 people the company lost on September 11. Tania would go there and sit on the granite bench and be with Dave. It always seemed to comfort her.

Linda took Tania's hand, and they walked the ten blocks to the memorial wall. They stood together in the plaza, and Tania brushed her hand over Dave's name. Before long, her tears stopped, and she seemed to be calming down. Linda stroked her friend's hair, knowing that Dave was bringing her peace.

"You can go home now, Linda," Tania said slowly. "I'm going to be all right."

Linda felt nauseous all the way home. When would enough ever be enough for her poor, tortured friend? she wondered. How could those people have been so mean to Tania? How could they have attacked her that way?

It was midafternoon when she finally got back to her apartment. Her telephone answering machine was blinking with a message. A reporter from the *New York Times* had called. They were doing a story on her friend, Tania Head, he said. Would she please give him a call?

THE *NEW YORK* *TIMES*

Every year, on the eve of the anniversary, Tania threw a party. Close friends gathered on the rooftop of her Manhattan apartment building to celebrate life before a somber day dedicated to reflection. It was supposed to be a festive event, and it always was. Dozens of people from the network, along with survivors from the Oklahoma City bombing, who in a show of solidarity traveled to ground zero every September, packed into the glass-enclosed party room overlooking Central Park. Tania was always the perfect host, mingling among the guests, filling empty wineglasses, and making sure that everyone's plate was piled high with picnic food. Like Linda always said, if a tragedy could spawn a celebrity, Tania was the World Trade Center superstar. It was never more evident than at her annual gathering, when guests angled to have a moment with her, and she basked in the attention.

This year was different.

The days leading up to the sixth anniversary were a spiral of emotion for Tania. She was increasingly agitated and withdrawn, snapping orders at people and sometimes not showing up where she was supposed to be. She often didn't take phone calls or return emails, and she wouldn't answer her door, even though it was obvious from the murmur of the TV that she was home. She was phoning her survivor friends three and four times a day, complaining that the *New York Times* reporter was stalking her for a story. As often as Tania had made it clear that she wasn't interested, she said—especially with her brother's death, and the anniversary looming—he was still snooping around, and she couldn't understand it. When Linda mentioned that a *Times* reporter had left her a message, Tania flew into a rage and made her swear not to return the call.

The whole thing confused Linda. She wondered why Tania was so upset, when she had certainly talked to reporters before. But even more perplexing was that, the way Tania told it, the *Times* reporter was circling around her like a blood-smelling shark. How could he be so insensitive, so cruel? Linda wondered. He might as well be pulling on the wings of a wounded bird. What the hell for? A fucking anniversary story?

Each time the *Times* called, Tania seemed to take another step backward. She began calling Richard Zimbler and Lori Mogol, her friends on the board, sometimes at two and three o'clock in the morning, carrying on about the invasion of her privacy. She complained bitterly that she felt the newspaper was on some kind of vendetta. They were probably piqued because she had changed her mind and backed out of interviews, she said. Now the reporter wouldn't stop calling, asking the same questions she'd already refused to answer. *What was Dave's last name? Where was he from? How had they met and when?* She didn't understand his insistence that she answer personal questions. Why did Dave's last name matter? He was her husband, and he was dead. End of story. None of the other reporters had pushed her to identify him—especially after she'd explained that his parents wanted to protect his privacy and their privacy. She had never gone against the wishes of her in-laws, and she wouldn't now, not even if the reporter called a hundred times a day.

By the night of the party, she was crippled with anxiety. While her guests were eating and drinking and admiring the sprawling view of the city, she was hunched alone in a corner outside on the terrace, clutching her cell phone. Every time someone approached her, she glowered and waved the person away. The guests began whispering among themselves:

"What's wrong with Tania?"

"It must be the anniversary."

"What can we do to help? Should we leave?"

"I'll take care of it," Linda said.

If ever there was a steadfast friend, it was Linda. Tania's cruelty toward her just kept escalating, yet she somehow managed to smile through the sarcasm and the mean jokes. Tania criticized her endlessly, from her choice of clothes, to the red color of her lipstick, to the way she wore her long, platinum blonde hair. Just that day, when she arrived early to help prepare for the party, Tania looked her over and asked with a sardonic grin, "Blondie, you're not really going to wear that tonight, are you?" Like all of the other times, Linda shook it off. She never knew whether she would find Tania the sweet, loving friend or her evil twin, and she'd learned to handle both. Some of the other survivors had criticized her for being a doormat for Tania and for fawning over her, but Linda didn't care what the others thought. As long as Tania needed her, she was going to be there. That's what friends did.

"Tania, honey, what's going on?" she asked, as Tania huddled in the corner of the terrace by herself.

Tania waved Linda away. "I don't want to talk about it," she hissed.

"Did they call again?" Linda asked. Tania glared at her and didn't answer. Speaking tentatively, Linda tried again. "Sweetie? Is that what it is? Did they just call?"

Linda sidled up to Tania and tried to console her, but Tania swatted at her. "Get away!" Tania cried. "Don't you know when to give up?"

Linda just sat there, watching Tania stare at her phone.

"Yes," Tania said finally. The reporter called again, and she'd hung up when she heard his voice. She barely had time to snap her cell phone shut when it rang again, but she let it go to voice mail. Tania was trembling. She couldn't take any more, she said, her thin lips quivering. She'd had it.

"Why are they *doing* this to me?" she wailed, while startled guests tried to act as if they hadn't heard her. "They're harassing me. After all I've been through, and they're harassing me!"

"What can I do to help, honey?" Linda asked, reaching for Tania's hand a second time.

"Leave me alone!" Tania cried, pounding her fist on her thigh. "Just leave me alone! I have to figure this out!"

Janice watched the scene between Tania and Linda from across the terrace. She had never seen Tania so hostile and recalcitrant. Watching her rocking back and forth, with her teeth clenched and her hand balled in a fist, she worried that Tania was finally cracking under the pressure.

"What's going on?" she asked as she approached Linda and Tania.

Linda explained about the *Times* and how aggressive the reporter had been calling Tania several times a day, pummeling her with questions, even after she had cancelled interviews and told them she was no longer interested in participating in their story. Tania was certain that he would call again any minute, and she was petrified.

"They're harassing her, Janice!" Linda said. "We've got to do something."

The survivors were always more susceptible to depression around the time of the anniversary, when images of the planes hitting the towers and the buildings falling down were replayed in the media and the whole world refocused its attention on the attacks. People who suffered from trauma often reacted in unpredictable ways, and Tania had experienced significant setbacks recently, such as the loss of her brother, and that terrible confrontation at the St. Regis Hotel with the angry families of her former coworkers. Her reaction to the reporter's phone calls was bizarre, Janice thought, until you took into consideration all of the other feelings she was coping with. Her overreaction was probably a culmination of emotions stemming from all of those things. Janice had always been Tania's voice of reason, and there was never a time she hadn't been able to reassure and console her back to composure. She was confident that this time would be no different.

Rubbing Tania's back, Janice spoke softly. "Why don't you just tell him that you'll talk to him after the anniversary is over?" she asked. "Just explain that this is a stressful time, and you'll be glad to call him when you're feeling better."

Tania erupted. "Because I don't want to talk to him, and I'm not going to talk to him," she said, seething. "Why is that so hard for you to understand?"

She had never snapped at Janice before. She was always reverential, in the way that a patient is with a counselor, or a child is with a parent. Her enmity told Janice that the woman was at her breaking point, and she had to do whatever she could to protect her.

"Give me the reporter's number," she said. "I'll call him and tell him to leave you alone."

As Tania sat there, rocking and crying, Janice dialed the *Times*. She explained to David Dunlap that she was with Tania and that Tania was very disturbed by his calls. Dunlap said he was sorry to have upset Tania, really he was, but he just didn't understand her reticence about answering basic questions he had. She had talked to other reporters on other anniversaries. What was so different now? The *Times*'s motive was no different than the others had been, Dunlap explained. They just wanted to write a profile of this brave, courageous survivor. The reporter's conciliatory tone did nothing to appease Janice. All she knew was that Tania was coming unhinged, and the *Times* apparently wasn't going away.

"You need to understand what these people go through," Janice said. "This is too stressful. The timing is bad. What is the purpose of this?"

"Why can't she just answer the questions?" Dunlap asked.

The telephone conversation quickly turned into a shouting match, with Janice ordering the reporter to back off and Dunlap insisting that Tania answer his questions. "I'll make a deal with you," Janice said finally. "If you leave her alone for now, I'll ask her to talk to you after the anniversary, and she can answer your questions then. We just need to get her through tomorrow. Okay?"

Dunlap promised he would be back in touch.

"Fuck him," Janice said, flipping her phone shut. "If he bothers you again, let me know."

Tania breathed a sigh of relief. She could always count on her inner circle to protect her. What Janice didn't know—what none of

the others at the party knew except for Tania—was that a day earlier, Dunlap had a similar conversation with Jennifer Adams, who
had suggested Tania in the first place, and the focus of his story had
taken a dramatic turn. Dunlap indicated that what began as an anniversary profile was turning into an investigation. Without giving
away too much, the reporter explained that Tania had cancelled three
in-person interviews, which seemed strange, and now she was refusing
to concede answers to the most elementary questions. His preliminary
reporting had turned up inconsistencies in her biography, and the
discrepancies needed to be cleared up whether the *Times* published a
story or not. Adams's instinct was to try to protect Tania, and she told
the *Times* to back off. She asked Dunlap to send her his questions,
and she would try to get answers. He did, that same afternoon, and
he had copied Tania on the email.

"Thank you so much for fielding these questions and for understanding that I mean no disrespect for Tania," the reporter wrote.
"With your help, I hope to put my concerns to rest and proceed with
a profile of an extraordinary, courageous, and generous survivor. The
details I'm asking here will simply fill in the background of her compelling personal narrative."

What followed were two pages of probing questions. Dunlap had
obviously done his homework.

"What was Dave's full name?" he asked. If Tania was, for some
reason, squeamish about having Dave's last name appear in print, the
reporter explained, that was an unusual request that he would have to
justify to his editors and readers.

"Was Dave her husband?" Dunlap asked. There was some confu-
sion, he said, because Tania had, at various times, to different people,
referred to him as both a husband and a fiancé.

"How long had Dave worked in the World Trade Center?" he
asked. "Where had she gone to school and what degree had she
earned? Did she attend school under a different name?"

Dunlap inquired as to whether Tania still worked for Merrill
Lynch, and asked whether her title was senior vice president for strategic alliances, "as noted on the WTCSN profile?"

"What was Tania doing in the south tower on the morning of Sept. 11, 2001?" he asked. "Also how long had she been hospitalized for her injuries and where? Is there a doctor or nurse who might attest to Tania's remarkable resiliency?" he wondered.

Dunlap concluded by apologizing for the intrusion into Tania's life, particularly on the eve of the anniversary. But, he explained, most of what he was looking for was basic biographical information that could be easily answered and would enhance the story he was writing.

Tania's party broke up early that night. Angelo was out of town, but his partner, Gabriel, was there, and when he tapped Tania on the shoulder to say good night, she swung around and looked at him as if he had struck her. Then Janice, whom he had always known to be a gentle spirit, lashed out. "It's not a good time," she snarled.

Inside, Linda thanked the guests for coming and explained why Tania was too distraught to say good-bye. The *New York Times* was harassing her for an interview, she said. The guests were aghast. How dare they do this on the eve of the anniversary!

A heavy, gray sky promised a grim backdrop for the sixth anniversary. It was the first time the anniversary had fallen on Tuesday, the same day of the week as the attacks, and the first time the ceremony had been held away from the site where the twin towers had once stood, across the street in Zuccotti Park. Tania wasn't going to attend, but, at the last minute, she decided to show up. She sat quietly with the other survivors, clutching a single pink rose that she had grabbed from one of the buckets of colored roses provided for the mourners. She was sulking. Every year, she had brought with her to the ceremony a toy yellow taxi in recognition of her first meeting with Dave and placed it near the reflecting pool in the footprint of the towers. This time, Elia, the survivor from Cuba who had escaped from both the 1993 and 2001 terrorist attacks, was supposed to get the car. There was a little place in Chinatown where she could buy it, and she'd promised to go there the day before. But that morning, in the Survivors' Network offices, just before they were ready to go to the service, Elia confessed that she had forgotten. Tania looked as if she'd stabbed her in the heart.

She summoned Linda, who volunteered to try to find one. Even though it wasn't yet eight in the morning, and most of the souvenir shops downtown had yet to open, Linda ran up and down Broadway searching for a toy yellow taxi. The best she had been able to come up with was a tiny cab dangling from a key chain. When she presented the key chain to Tania, sheepishly explaining that it was all she could find at that early hour, Tania growled and grabbed the key chain, throwing it against the wall in a fit of rage. "This is not what I wanted!" she screamed. Linda and Elia both jumped back, startled by her reaction. They feared that their leader was about to shatter, and there didn't seem to be anything anyone could say or do to shake her out of her funk.

The ceremony began as it always did, with the unfurling of a torn American flag that had been salvaged from ground zero, and a moment of silence at precisely 8:46 a.m. when the first plane had hit. People jammed together in the drizzle, holding framed photographs and other mementos of lost loved ones. When a children's choir finished singing the national anthem, Mayor Michael Bloomberg walked to the podium and stirred the crowd with thoughtful words.

"That day we felt isolated, but not for long and not from each other," he said, as dignitaries such as Senator Hillary Clinton, former mayor Rudy Giuliani, and New York governor Eliot Spitzer looked on. "Six years have passed, and our place is still by your side." The program commenced with the reading of the names of the 2,750 dead by some of the firefighters and rescuers who had helped save thousands on that day. Tears streamed down Tania's cheeks when Dave's name was read.

The gray sky gave way to pelting rain as hundreds of family members and survivors walked from the park, across the street to the place where the towers once stood, and down a long ramp to the reflecting pool, seven stories below ground level. Tania walked alone behind Linda, Elia, Janice, and the others in her group. Linda couldn't help but think how destroyed her friend looked, slumped over and soaking wet, with her white blouse stuck to her and her short hair matted to her head. As people took turns dropping roses in the reflecting pool and moving on, Tania stood still, clutching her rose to her chest. She seemed to be somewhere else. Linda wondered where.

By the end of the four-hour ceremony, the rain had slowed to a trickle. A knot of stragglers lingered as the trumpeters played "Taps." Tania's friends looked over at her. She looked beyond miserable. "What can I do?" Janice asked gently, walking up behind her. Tania swung around. "I can't take this!" she cried, shoving her cell phone toward the clutch of survivors who remained. "They won't leave me alone! The reporters! They just won't leave me alone!" Janice stood there, stunned. She had thought that Tania was overcome with terrible memories and missing Dave. But she hadn't even mentioned her husband. She was still worrying about the damn newspaper interview. The relentless pressure from the *Times* had obviously sent Tania into a perilous emotional spiral.

"My God, Tania," Janice said. "You don't have to talk to anyone if you don't want to. If you're feeling that they're harassing you, why don't you call a lawyer? This way, you'll know what your rights are. I'll even go with you."

Tania's face was red and blotchy, and her hands shook. "Leave me alone!" she shouted. "I'll take care of this. Stop interfering! Just leave me alone."

"We're only trying to help you," Linda said, trying to get Tania to calm down.

"I don't need your help!" Tania fumed, pushing past Janice.

The others looked on, bewildered. "What's wrong with you?" Janice cried. "I'm trying to help you. Please, just let me help you."

"I said leave me alone!" Tania screamed. "All of you! Just leave me alone!"

And then she was gone.

As the survivors suffered through their anniversary with Tania, Angelo was sitting, of all places, in the Bob Barker Studios in Hollywood, California.

"Angelo Guglielmo! Come on down! You're the next contestant on *The Price Is Right!*" the announcer shouted over the loudspeakers. It was a quick appearance, and as he left the soundstage with his winnings—a birdbath—his cell phone rang. Gabriel was calling.

"Angelo," he said, "you need to come back to New York. Something is terribly wrong with Tania."

UNRAVELING

Tania's friends were tiring of her frantic calls about the *Times* story. The paper was out to get her, she said, and she didn't understand why. It was David against Goliath. One of the largest news organizations in the world was going to write lies, and there was nothing she could do to stop it. She passed around copies of the questions in Dunlap's email. What was Dave's last name? What was she doing on the ninety-sixth floor? What was her alma mater? Did she work for Merrill Lynch? How dare he question the veracity of her story!

Her friends were puzzled.

"Tania, why are you so upset?" Elia asked after reading Dunlap's questions. "Everything he wants to know is verifiable. Get Dave's parents to talk to him. Dave's friends. Have Merrill Lynch verify that you work there. There is nothing to worry about."

Tania couldn't be mollified. She dispatched Janice to the *Times*'s offices to appeal directly to the staff. Dunlap listened politely as Janice explained that Tania was going through hell and didn't want them to write about her. "I don't think it did any good," she told Tania after she left the newspaper that day.

Linda begged Tania to let her help. "Give me some evidence that I can bring to the *Times*," she said. "Give me the name of the firefighter that carried you out that morning. The one that you were handed off to, that carried you out and threw you under that fire truck when the tower came down, right on West Street. You told me that story a million times. He can verify your story. Give me his name so I can bring it to the *Times*."

Tania refused.

On Friday, September 21, she called Janice to say that she had made an appointment with a lawyer. Would she please come? That afternoon, Janice took the train from her home in Seaford, Long Island, and met Tania outside the attorney's office on the Avenue of the Americas in Midtown Manhattan. She was surprised to see someone else—a person she had never seen before—with her. Tania introduced the woman as her mother. An obviously well-heeled woman who was neatly groomed and wearing a conservative business suit, she seemed to be shy and spoke broken English.

Inside the office tower, the three women boarded the elevator. Tania giggled nervously.

"I have a confession to make," she said when the elevator doors closed.

"What is it?" Janice asked.

"I'm not a US citizen."

Janice looked at Tania, waiting for the punch line.

"Don't you understand?" Tania asked. She suddenly seemed like the old Tania. Sweet and funny and childlike.

"Understand?" Janice asked.

The reason that she had been avoiding the *Times* and didn't want to speak to the reporter, Tania explained, was that she wasn't a US citizen, and she feared the newspaper would reveal that in its story. She could lose her job or, worse yet, be deported if all of her papers weren't in order. It took a minute for what Tania had said to register, but when it did, Janice started to laugh. It suddenly all made sense. The bizarre behavior of late. The growing anxiety every time the paper called. Tania had a secret, and she was afraid of what the *Times* would do with it.

"That's what all of this is about?" Janice cried. "That you're not a US citizen? Oh, Tania! No one is going to care that you're not a citizen."

Tania took a deep breath and smiled. Her mother shook her head up and down, but she didn't seem to understand. "No *importa*," Tania said.

The law firm of Furgang & Adwar occupied a plush suite of offices on the twenty-eighth floor filled with mahogany furniture, marble

statuary, and paintings that looked like they belonged in the Metropolitan Museum of Art. Stephanie Furgang Adwar was a high-priced
entertainment attorney with offices in midtown, West Nyack, and
White Plains. Janice figured she must be an acquaintance of Tania's
family. Adwar was a good-looking woman with a firm, confident
handshake.

"I'm sorry," she said, pumping Janice's hand, "but you're not family, so you won't be able to come into the meeting."

"No problem," Janice said. "I'm just here as her friend. To be supportive."

The door closed behind Tania and her mother, and Janice picked
up a magazine and began leafing through it. She couldn't help
but smile thinking about what Tania had just said. "I'm not a US
citizen." She had looked like a child in trouble when she made her
big confession. All these weeks, the poor woman had put herself
through hell because she was afraid that the *Times* would reveal
she wasn't a citizen—as if that meant anything in the context of
her incredible story of courage and survival. Janice felt even more
determined to help Tania understand that, in fact, she was moving
forward, and that irrational fears, while debilitating and to be overcome, were an inevitable part of healing.

Two hours passed, maybe a little less. The door to Adwar's office
swung open, and the lawyer smiled warmly and invited Janice inside.
Janice joined Tania and her mother at a long conference table. As she
pulled up a chair, Tania looked at her with a strange gaze. "Are you
mad at me?" she asked. Janice was puzzled by the question.

"Why would I be mad at you?" Tania didn't respond.

Adwar seemed to be in a hurry and remained standing while she
spoke. "You know, Tania, that it's okay that you didn't really work in
the World Trade Center but had only been visiting when the terrorist
attack happened, right?" the lawyer asked. "And you know that no
one will hold it against you that you only knew Dave for a couple of
months and weren't married to him, right?"

Janice was confused. "What the hell is this woman talking about?"

"And no one is going to hold it against you that you embellished a few things here and there. You know that, Tania, right? Everyone tells a white lie now and then."

Tania gazed at the attorney but said nothing. She reached for a candy in a bowl on the conference table. For a moment, the only sound in the room was the crinkling of the cellophane wrapper. Janice's brain raced with questions. Tania hadn't actually worked in the Trade Center? She wasn't married to Dave? Embellishing? White lies?

The enormity of what the lawyer was saying suddenly hit her like a boulder falling from the sky, and she gasped. "I can't believe what I'm hearing," she said to herself. "Tania is lying? She has been lying to all of these people for all of this time? Suddenly, everything Tania had ever told Janice was suspect. Janice even doubted the little bits of her story Tania clung to in the lawyer's office. There wasn't an executive job in the south tower? Was there no Dave? No storybook meeting in a New York City cab? No wedding? This can't be." Janice felt the blood drain from her face. The lawyer was speaking again, but her words blurred into background noise.

If Dave was a figment of Tania's imagination, had there really been an assistant who'd lost her life in the sky lobby? Had there been a dying man who'd begged her to take his wedding ring and return it to his wife? And had Welles Remy Crowther, one of the great heroes of the September 11 tragedy, really saved Tania?

"My God," Janice thought, "I went with her to meet that young man's family. I sat with them at dinner in the Princeton Club and listened to her promise to send them a piece of her burned clothing because it was one of the last things their son had ever touched. I listened as they thanked her, from the bottom of their hearts, for sharing the story of their boy's heroics, and asked her to speak at his memorial. I heard her badger Linda into delivering her speech and then watched her cry with Jeff Crowther at that memorial."

Had Tania even been at the World Trade Center that day? Her story had been so horrific that no one had ever thought to question it. Not her new friends who had spent countless hours crying with her, not the media that had written so many accounts of her survival, and not the politicians who lauded her for her courage. Besides, Tania said that she had been gravely injured in the attack, and she *did* have the scars on her arm.

Janice suddenly felt sick. A fist to the stomach. She was overcome with forbidding thoughts. It was too much, and she had to get away. She thanked the attorney for her time and slowly rose to her feet to leave. She felt wobbly as she walked out of the office, and she was so distracted she didn't even realize that Tania and her mother had followed her back into the elevator. No one spoke at first. Janice wasn't sure she could find the words even if she wanted to say something.

Then Tania piped up, "Want to go get something to eat?"

Janice was incredulous. She wanted to scream but managed to keep her composure. She needed to escape, to try to make sense of what she'd just heard. "No, I've got to get home," she said.

The three women stepped out onto the busy city street, said hasty good-byes, and Janice headed for the train station. But before she had gotten too far, she heard Tania's mother say to her, "I don't understand. I told her not to do these things."

Janice boarded the train back to Seaford and lost herself in a labyrinth of thoughts. She returned to conversations with Tania, sometimes at two and three in the morning, and talking to her the way a mother would a daughter until she was finally able to fall asleep. Her mind drifted to Lee Ielpi, and how he had entrusted Tania with representing his beloved son on tours of the sacred ground where Jonathan had given his life. She thought about the survivors, whose faith in humanity had been shattered but who had risked trusting again and had chosen Tania to lead them out of the abyss. She thought about Linda, dear Linda, and how she had unselfishly devoted herself to Tania at the monumental expense of helping herself.

"How could Tania have done this?" Janice asked herself. "How could she have betrayed so many people who had been through so much? And for God's sake, why?" She had chosen the most vulnerable people and exploited them by making up a tale so terribly heartbreaking that they couldn't do anything but trust her and care for her— care for her more than they'd cared for themselves—because her story was the saddest of them all. Except that now she doubted it had even happened. Was all a lie?

For four years, Tania had been telling her story, and no one had questioned the validity of it until now. There had been signs along the way, little discrepancies that everyone, herself included, had been almost too willing to overlook. "Why?" she wondered as the train chugged toward Seaford. Why hadn't she ever stopped Tania when she referred to Dave as her fiancé rather than her husband? Why hadn't she pushed to see the house in Amagansett after Tania had made and then broken so many promises to take her there? Why had she never insisted on seeing the burned jacket? Had she wanted that badly for Tania's story to be true?

Janice missed her stop that night. She never even heard the conductor announce the Seaford station. When she finally got home, she sat alone in the dark for hours, wondering how to break the news to Linda and the other survivors. Would they even believe her when she told them that the woman who had been there for them—who had turned herself over to them, nurturing them and rallying them and teaching them by example how to transcend their unimaginable sorrow, who had also taken as much as she had given—may never have been there at all.

THE TRUTH REVEALED

Janice hardly slept that night. She tossed and turned as the hours passed, thinking about how to tell the others what she knew. These were people who had been torn apart by tragedy and were mended only tenuously by the thread of trust they had in one another. When they learned that the most devout among them had violated that oath of faith, and so egregiously, would the thread snap?

Linda was of most concern. When she first joined the group, she was broken, and she had invested so much of her energy in Tania that she'd often neglected to take care of herself. Tania was her best friend. Her mentor. Her reason for being when there wasn't much else. She often told people that Tania had taught her how to live with dignity. How would she possibly react when she learned that she had entrusted her heart to a woman who wasn't there?

Janice dialed Linda's number, and she answered on the first ring.

"Are you sitting down?" Janice asked.

"Yes," Linda said, her voice bright and singsongy. "I'm sitting at my kitchen table, having my first cup of coffee."

"There's something I need to tell you."

People in the survivors' circle were always playing little jokes on one another, and Janice, more than most, loved pranks. Linda waited to hear more.

"Tania's a fraud," Janice said.

Linda giggled politely, but she didn't think this little joke was funny. Not at all.

"I'm sorry to be the one to tell you this," Janice said. Linda could hear the tremor in her friend's voice.

"Come on, Janice," she said. "She's not a fraud. What are you talking about?"

Janice went on to describe the scene in the lawyer's office the day before, and how Tania had all but admitted that there had been no husband named Dave or sprawling office in the twin towers with a full staff. Listening with disbelief, Linda sank deeper and deeper in her chair. She just couldn't get her head around what Janice was saying. She needed time to think. To decide whether she even believed what she was hearing.

When the women hung up, Linda went to her couch, where she spent the remainder of the morning staring out her living room window and feeling nothing but numbness. All of a sudden, it just made sense. All of the inconsistencies that everyone in their inner circle— Brendan and Janice and Elia and Gerry—relegated to Tania's trauma. Sometimes she called Dave her husband. Other times, she referred to him as her fiancé. The fact that no one ever met Dave's parents or even saw them with her at an anniversary. Her coworkers who were never around. Elvis the golden retriever. She had always said the dog was with her housekeeper, Lupe, at the beach house in Amagansett. Yet as often as she had promised to take Linda there, she had always come up with last-minute excuses. In a strange and bizarre way, it all seemed to add up to what Janice was saying. Tania was an imposter.

Meanwhile, Janice dialed Dunlap at the *Times*. For weeks, she and the others had stonewalled the reporter and vilified him to one another, when all he had been trying to do was get at the truth. He obviously had suspicions about Tania's story, and she realized how foolish she must have seemed in her blind defense of her. At the time, she thought she was doing the right thing, protecting a lamb from being preyed upon. She owed it to Dunlap, and she owed it to the survivors, to make things right.

The reporter answered his phone.

"This is Janice Cilento," she said. "I hate doing this, but I wanted to call you to say that I think Tania has been lying."

"You're doing the right thing," he said.

The rest of the Survivors' Network board took the news with disbelief. Elia was at her desk at the Port Authority when the call came from Linda.

"It's about Tania," Linda said.

Elia began screaming and crying, bringing her coworkers to her side. Her first thought was that Tania had died.

"What is it?" she cried. "What's happened? Did she do something to herself?"

"It's not what you think," Linda said. "It's not what you think. Tania . . . Tania is a fraud."

Elia felt nauseous. Her first inclination was to scream at Linda. How dare she say such a terrible thing? But, way down, in the place in her gut that never lied, she knew what Linda was saying was the truth. All she could do was cry.

Only Brendan Chellis breathed a sigh of relief when he heard. For months, he had kept his suspicions to himself as he watched Tania bask in her celebrity and suck the life out of his friends with her constant bids for attention. So when Richard Zimbler and Lori Mogol called, their voices grave, and said they had something to tell him about Tania, he felt like a weight had been lifted off his chest.

"I already know," he said.

For the next few days, as the *Times* wrapped up its research, Tania's friends took her calls, acting as if nothing had changed. They didn't want to tip her off that the story was about to break. She had taken a short sabbatical to Spain with her mother, but Janice spoke to her every day, trying to encourage her to weigh in should a story be published. She finally agreed to a three-way conference call with Janice and *Times* investigative reporter Serge Kovaleski. The call lasted about thirty minutes, with Kovaleski asking questions and Tania skirting around them. In her reticence, she would say only that she had done nothing illegal.

The reporter finally spelled it out for her. Her lack of clarity had gone on long enough, and their story was nearing completion. They really wanted her to have her say, but time was running short. Tania promised to meet with Kovaleski when she returned from Spain. But once again, she cancelled.

On the eve of publication, Tania wrote a blanket email to her survivor friends:

> As you know, the *New York Times* is going to publish an article about me. I ask all of you to please not listen to what is in the article, but reflect upon what you know of me.

On September 27, 2007, the headline on the front page of the *Times* read, "In a 9/11 Survival Tale, the Pieces Just Don't Fit." A photograph of Tania leading the Tribute Center tour for Pataki, Bloomberg, and Giuliani accompanied the 2,200-word account. The story quoted almost everyone on the Survivors' Network board and deconstructed Tania's personal history, myth by myth: The family of Dave ██████ ████████, the man she claimed to have married, who really did die in the north tower, had never heard of a Tania Head. Merrill Lynch had no record of an employee with her name. Nor did Harvard or Stanford have a Tania Head in its student files.

"In recent weeks, the *New York Times* sought to interview Ms. Head about her experiences on 9/11 because she had, in other settings, presented a poignant account of survival and loss," the story said. "But she cancelled three scheduled interviews, citing her privacy and emotional turmoil, and declined to provide details to corroborate her story.

"Indeed," the *Times* concluded, "no part of her story has been verified."

The Survivors' Network board held an emergency meeting to vote Tania out of the organization and to appoint Richard Zimbler as acting president. The board released a statement:

> Tania Head is no longer associated with the World Trade Center Survivors' Network. This change will have no impact on the WTCSN's mission or effectiveness. We are on track and moving forward to ensure that the people in our community get the services they need. Our organization was created so that those af-

fected by the terrorist attacks could help each other through crisis and its aftermath. That mission, as well as the bond of fellowship we share with the other members of the 9/11 Community, remains unchanged.

Officials of the Tribute Center issued their own statement saying that Tania would no longer participate in the docent program. "At this time, we are unable to confirm the veracity of her connection to the events of September 11," Jennifer Adams told the *Times*.

No one felt more vindicated by the revelations than Gerry Bogacz. He remembered once asking Tania for her husband's last name, then going home to look him up in the roll of the World Trade Center dead. He wasn't sure why he had even asked, but he wondered if Tania had picked up on some doubt that he wasn't even conscious of at the time. He'd found Dave's name and never gave the incident a second thought. But, thinking back, he remembered that his troubles with the board began soon after that.

Just before the *Times* outed her, Tania had called Bogacz's office and begged him not to speak to the reporters about her. It was the first time he had heard from her since he'd been driven out of the survivors' group, and her call had come too late, even if he had been inclined to grant her request, which he wasn't. He had already spoken with the *Times*.

"No," he had said. "I won't promise you that. The only thing I promise is to answer their questions with the truth."

THE
AFTERMATH

The board sent Tania a certified letter making her removal from the group official.

"The board of the World Trade Center Survivors' Network (WTCSN) voted to remove you as president and revoke your membership. Therefore, please immediately return to our office at 22 Cortlandt Street all documents, records, and property related to the formation, governance, membership, and operations of this organization and its affiliated online groups, including financial records, passwords, membership lists, and the corporate seal."

The letter came back unopened and stamped "Unclaimed."

Tania seemed to have vanished.

What she'd done that ill-fated day is hijack a defenseless people and shake their faith in the goodness of mankind. Yet the great irony was that she had also taught by example that healing from such a terrible breach of trust came with taking care of one another.

The Survivors' Network went into damage control with the collective resilience of troops goaded into battle. Was its aggressive defense a fight-or-flight reaction to yet another crushing event in the members' lives, or was it that they had simply learned from the best? Probably a combination of both. Saving their trademark meant saving themselves. There was work to be done.

With a measured, almost philosophical resolve, Acting President Richard Zimbler drove the message that the network was intact and continuing to work toward its core mission. The media frenzy was daunting, but the outpouring of support from leaders in the 9/11 community was encouraging. Alice Greenwald, the director of the

National September 11 Memorial Museum (then known as the World Trade Center Memorial Museum), assured the survivors that their involvement in the planning process would continue. Jennifer Adams promised continued solidarity with the Tribute Center. The survivors focused their attention on the network's goals. Linda Gormley and Gerry Bogacz met with museum curators to help guide the plans for the Survivors' Stairway to what would be its permanent place in the underground memorial museum. Elia Zedeño and Peter Miller lectured at schools and colleges when requests came into the Survivors' Speaker's Bureau.

"Part of the reason why I was in pain after I found out that she lied was because I felt that I'd just buried another friend as a result of September 11," Elia Zedeño said, speaking sadly but with resolution. "So it was basically a matter of, this is a funeral. My erasing her from my future is, well, I buried a friend."

As expected, Linda Gormley was hit hardest by the revelations of Tania's deceit, and her rage was palpable.

"I'm going to make it my mission that she never do this to anyone else in any other tragedy," she said. "Tania was my idol. She was the person I looked up to. But she wasn't real. It wasn't real. I have no place in my heart at this moment to forgive her. What she did is unforgivable. This country was attacked by terrorists. We lost almost three thousand people on September 11, and what this woman did was terrorism to me. Should we forgive the terrorists? No. I look at her as no more than a terrorist from September 11."

Tania had deceived many during her nearly five-year reign as America's most famous survivor. None had been more supportive of her than her band of supporters from the Oklahoma City tragedy. Richard Williams reached out to her on behalf of himself, his wife, Lynne, and the others from their circle who had come to know Tania so well. In his quest for the truth, he wrote her a letter and asked the question that everyone wanted answered:

> I haven't said much during this last two weeks, but I really wanted you to know how all of these revelations affected me. First of all,

I want you to know that I still hold very dear that person who laughed with us through Chinatown and Little Italy, and shared the sights and sounds of Manhattan. I want very badly to believe that the real person I felt I knew is somewhere under all of the reports we've heard recently. We felt such a personal tie with you when you allowed us to share in those things. You must realize that as forsaken as you must feel, we feel equally forsaken. We've loved you—not because of your injuries, your marriage, your job, or your social status—we've loved you because you captured our hearts on a personal level. I don't want to lose a friendship because we can't be completely truthful with each other. Please tell us the one thing that we really need to know. Were you in the towers on 9/11/01? Please?

AN ENDING FOR THE MOVIE

"Sometimes," she said, "I have to go back and think, 'Was it real? Was it a dream? Was my life really like that? Or was it just all make-believe?'"

—Tania talking about her life, and all the sadness
she had endured since September 11, 2001

I had just gotten back from my trip to LA and quickly read the *Times* article in the morning, then headed for Tania's apartment. Pushing past the reporters outside, I rushed through the lobby and took the elevator to apartment 1803. Tania was alone. She was disheveled in a T-shirt and sweatpants and obviously stunned by what was happening.

She had read the story and seen the initial television reports, some of which included interviews with members of the Survivors' Network board. Gerry. Richard. Janice. Linda. Tania was furious at Linda for talking to the *Times* but the interview that sent her into a tailspin was the one by Janice, who had gone on camera for *Good Morning America*. The piece was introduced by Diane Sawyer and narrated by Chris Cuomo, and in it Janice says, "I've heard her story over and over. I've been there any time she needed someone to listen, even if it was at three in the morning. She has stolen my time and my soul. All I know is, for the last four years, she's been lying to me, and I feel betrayed."

Janice felt betrayed? Tania was incredulous. "How could she say she's my friend and say these things?" she asked. Gerry Bogacz appeared in the same segment. He said he was "shaken" by the revelations in the *Times*. She could almost understand Gerry speaking to the press, she said. But Janice was her "New York mom."

"I never thought . . . Janice? . . . Never!" she cried.

For the hour or so that I was there, Tania toggled between rage and self-pity. One minute her face was twisted in a scowl. The next, her lips quivered, and her eyes brimmed with tears. "How could they say all these terrible things about me?" she asked. "What kind of friends are these?"

I couldn't help but feel sad for her. She seemed genuinely bewildered, and, at the same time, she seemed to be searching desperately for a way to stay connected to the world that was slipping away. "No one is talking to me," she said. "No one is answering their phone." Her own phone was ringing nonstop. She kept checking her caller ID before taking any calls. I assumed that most of those she answered were from relatives in Spain who had heard about what was happening. The constant interruptions made it hard to get what I had come there for: the truth. But I felt I had to try. At that point, my allegiance was with the true survivors. They were reeling, and I wanted to be able to offer them some explanation about why she did what she did, or, even better, to deliver an apology or heartfelt words of regret.

I was caught in a flurry of emotions because I still cared about Tania. I suppose that the enormity of what she'd done—who she really was—just hadn't hit me yet. I'd be lying if I said I hadn't given any thought to the impact this spectacular turn of events would have on the survivors' documentary. I had hours of Tania on video, talking about every aspect of her survivor's story. I asked her to go on camera then and there to address the accusations against her. I told her she could say whatever she wanted.

"This is your opportunity to set the record straight," I said.

"No!" she said, swinging from tears to fury. "Is the camera on?" she asked.

I told her it wasn't. She went to check my camera bag, convinced that I was pulling a fast one. "You know I wouldn't do that," I said.

"They're hypocrites!" she cried, satisfied that I wasn't recording her surreptitiously. "Every last one of them. I helped a lot of people. Did they forget that?"

At that moment, it became clear that I was seeing two personalities coming together. I didn't detect a trace of remorse from either one. Tania played me a phone message from one of the Oklahoma City survivors. "We're sticking with you, kid," the woman on the message said. "We're not going anywhere." She snapped her phone shut. "These are friends!" she cried, shaking the phone in her clenched fist. "These are real friends!"

I stayed for a while longer, waiting patiently as she fielded calls, unable to understand most of what she was saying because she spoke in Spanish. I realized that my mission had been futile. I wasn't going to learn, as I'd hoped, that Tania was telling the truth, that the *Times* had gotten it all wrong. And I wasn't going to get a confession of guilt, not by any means. There would be no clarity for me that day.

As I prepared to leave, I embraced her. "I'm so sorry this is happening to you," I said. I pulled on my jacket, and she turned toward me, gazing into my eyes, her own dark eyes so penetrating that I felt as though she were hacking into my consciousness. But her words didn't match my thoughts. She didn't say anything about sadness or regret, or shattered trust and broken hearts. She was oddly pragmatic.

"Well," she said. "Now we have an ending for the movie." Her answer, and the matter-of-fact way in which she delivered it, gave me the chills. Yet, in a strange way, I understood what she meant.

My filmmaker instincts kicked into high gear after that. I called the survivors with whom I had been working and asked each of them how they wanted to proceed with the documentary, if they wanted to proceed at all.

They took a vote and unanimously decided that they wished to see it finished. Their goal in taking part in the movie was always that the true story be told, warts and all, and Tania's role, whatever it turned out to be, was crucial to that narrative. I appreciated their trust.

Tania, meanwhile, simply disappeared. Some of the survivors said that she had made limp attempts at contacting them, but only Brendan Chellis responded. In her email to him, Tania wrote, "Can you tell me where you stand in regards to me? Do you want to talk to me or not and hear what I have to say?" I was shocked to learn that Brendan had been onto Tania for months before the *Times* story, but he had said nothing for fear of being abandoned by the group. After her email, he had a phone conversation with her that went pretty much the way my visit with her had. Tania stuck to her story and claimed that the media was out to get her. How could her friends have turned against her the way they did? She couldn't understand it.

Of all of the survivors, I worried most about Linda. Tania had been the sister that Linda never had. She had shared her most intimate thoughts with Tania. The sense of betrayal she must have felt had to have been overwhelming. When I checked in on her a few weeks after Tania was exposed, she told me that she was suffering from debilitating panic attacks and nightmares—all of the symptoms she suffered right after 9/11. She told me she felt terrorized all over again. Wavering between rage and fear, Linda vowed to do whatever she could to make sure that no one else fell under Tania's spell. Taking part in the documentary was a way for her to do that.

Late that fall, as filming for the documentary resumed, Tania called me out of the blue. She was panic-stricken.

"Are you going forward with the movie?" she asked. Her voice cracked, and she sounded as if she was on the verge of hysteria.

I decided to tell her the truth. That I was making the film.

"How could you do this to me, Angelo?" she cried.

"Tania," I said, calmly, "this is what you've always wanted. You were the one who wanted a survivors' movie. I started it for you, and the others want it finished."

She was furious. She huffed and seethed and threatened me with repercussions. I struggled with the pity I felt for her. It was tough. I promised I wouldn't demonize her.

"And how will you do that?" she asked, her voice now engaged and curious.

"By telling the truth," I said. "But also showing all the good that you did, too."

I encouraged Tania to come clean. No matter how ugly the truth might be. I truly believed that a public telling of her side of the story, and an apology to the people she'd betrayed, if that was what was called for, would help her. She wouldn't hear of it.

"I want the footage," she said.

"It's not my footage to give," I said. "It belongs to the Survivors' Network. You know that."

She flew into a rage. "One day the truth will come out, and you'll all feel terrible and apologize to me," she said.

I wanted so much to believe that the story would turn out that way, but the person I saw after the story broke wasn't the Tania I had known and cared for. She was harder, calculating, and bitter. I wanted the old Tania back. But even more than that, I wanted to know her the way she knew me. I wanted her to be as revealing as she had been on camera when I interviewed her for the original survivors' documentary—before her real identity was revealed. Only this time, she would be telling the truth. But that was not to be. Finally, I realized that if I were ever going to get answers, I would have to find them on my own.

In order to flush out the end of the story, I had to start at the beginning. My search took me to Spain, where I spent the entire month of July talking to anyone who could help me figure out who the real Tania was. Working with local professionals—a detective, a producer, and a reporter from the Spanish newspaper *La Vanguardia*—I collected many pieces to the puzzle.

Tania's lies began with her name. It is Alicia Esteve Head. Her mother, Acacia Head Ledeveze, the granddaughter of the British consulate to the Canary Islands, was working as a flight attendant for British Airways when she met Francisco Esteve Corbella, a wealthy Spanish businessman thirteen years her senior. They married and had five children. Alicia, born on July 31, 1973, is the youngest and the only girl. The family lived a prosperous life, traversing among their

sprawling Barcelona apartment on the Calle dels Vergós, a three-story
villa in Majorca with a balcony overlooking the Mediterranean Sea,
and a country estate they named *El Campesino*. Their social circle
included powerful politicians and European royalty, and family life
revolved around yachting and horses and tennis at exclusive country
clubs.

It was no surprise to me that Tania/Alicia grew up in lavish sur-
roundings. Driving a rented Vespa through the neighborhoods of her
childhood in Barcelona, I recalled conversations where she described
the places I was seeing. The city was filled with Antonio Gaudi's magnificent architecture. It occurred to me that Gaudi's creations had the
same dimensions of her imagination: epic in scale and a perspective
all its own.

Many of the people I met with in Barcelona were wary of talking
at first. After the story broke, Alicia's mother, who owns a haber-
dashery shop in the city, appealed to friends not to speak to anyone
about her daughter. Those who did eventually open up about what
they knew did so only on the condition that their names wouldn't
be used. They said they did not want to be associated with such a sad
story. Sonia Humet was an exception. We flew to Slovakia to film her.
Alicia's best friend from childhood spoke openly, she said, because she
wanted people to know there was more to Alicia than what was written in the media.

Sonia met Alicia when both were six or seven and attending the
Canigó School, a rich and conservative Opus Dei Catholic school in
Barcelona. She said that even back then, Alicia idolized Americans
and hung a huge American flag in her bedroom in Barcelona. Alicia
"always had a problem with her imagination," Sonia said. When she
was frustrated or bored with the direction of her life, she simply made
up stories to accommodate her fantasy existence. Her tales, usually
about boyfriends and dating, were harmless enough and not atypical
for a teenage girl. But she earned a reputation as a storyteller and was
sometimes subject to the cruelties of other adolescents who laughed at
her tall tales and also chided her about being overweight. When Sonia
accused her of telling fairy tales, Alicia would become angry and shut

down. Sonia eventually allowed her imaginary lapses, never again questioning her stories, and they remained the best of friends until Alicia left for Switzerland to attend high school at an exclusive private boarding school.

It was after she returned to Barcelona to study at European University that Alicia's life took a vicious twist. She was eighteen and traveling in a car with a group of friends along the Valencia coast when the driver, fiddling with a music cassette tape, according to Sonia, lost control of the car. The vehicle crashed into a wall and rolled over several times before finally coming to a stop. Alicia was the most seriously hurt. Her right arm was severed and thrown from the vehicle. The story that her family told, which is hard to imagine, was that when help arrived, she was found holding the arm. The extremity was sewn back on, and, in the following months, Alicia underwent multiple surgeries at the famous Mayo Clinic in Minnesota, eventually regaining some use of the limb.

Her hard luck continued when, in the summer of 1992, her father and oldest brother, Francisco Javier Esteve Head were accused of embezzlement in the infamous and highly publicized £24 million Planasdemunt financial scandal in Catalonia and served short prison terms, spilling shame on the Esteve family name. Her parents' marriage fell apart, and Alicia and her mother grew estranged from her father and brothers. The unraveling of what she portrayed as her perfect home life seemed to be her undoing. It is around that time, after those life-changing events, and especially after her family unit fractured following her parents' contentious divorce, that Alicia started living in make-believe worlds.

The young woman had just begun her second and final year in the MBA program at the business school Esade when the World Trade Center was attacked. The school was closed on September 11, 2001, when Catalonia celebrated La Diada, its national independence day. But Alicia was back with her classmates when school resumed in mid-September. After speaking to people from Esade, I realized that there was no way she could have been in New York on 9/11, much less in the towers. A representative from Esade business school said that Alicia did not take a leave of absence from school that month. Her classmates said she never mentioned being involved in the attack, and they saw no evidence of injuries. Indeed, on a day when she claimed to be still in a coma in a New York City hospital burn unit, with Lauren Manning as her roommate, Alicia was in a classroom in Barcelona, taking a mandatory test for school. Lauren said neither she nor her husband have ever met or even heard of Tania Head or an Alicia Esteve Head.

In May 2002, Alicia graduated from business school with her MBA. She told classmates that Barcelona wasn't big enough for her dreams and she was going to New York City to start a new life. One year later, having studied everything that was written about September 11, Alicia Esteve Head became Tania Head. Three months after that, she was on her way to becoming America's most famous survivor.

September 11, 2008, was a turning point for the survivors. With Tania gone, Linda did most of the planning for the seventh anniversary in 2008, and everything went seamlessly. I stood from a distance with my camera and, for the first time, rather than focus all of their emotions on Tania, I saw that the survivors were free to feel their own feelings, as poignant and painful as those feelings were. Still, after all that had transpired, after all of the heartache she had caused them, Tania was never far from their thoughts.

Through the enormous crowd of mourners, I glanced over at Linda and Elia, walking up the ramp from the footprints of the towers, locking arms, wiping away tears. I knew they were tears for Tania. "Why do I feel this way?" Linda asked Elia. "It's not fair. I miss her!" Elia smiled. "Me too," she said.

Later, Elia summed up what we were all feeling: "Part of the sadness I feel was that someone who I got to love was no longer with us," she said. "And it hurt, even though I don't want that person around anymore. I hated the feeling. Because I don't want to miss her. But she became a part of our lives."

The World Trade Center Survivors' Network continues to advocate for the people whose lives were spared on September 11. Linda, Elia, and Janice all serve on the board. Richard Zimbler is president. Gerry Bogacz is cochairman of the group 9/11 Community for Common Ground Initiative, an organization formed to heal the divisions between religious and ethnic groups that have arisen from or been exacerbated by the terrorist attacks of September 11, 2001.

Alicia continues to travel between New York City and Barcelona, trying to keep a low profile. She has not had any contact with the survivors since they expelled her from the network, but they are suspicious of the origins of mysterious posts on the forum admonishing the survivors for not forgiving their former leader and for claiming that she had killed herself. The survivors believe those anonymous posts were from Tania. She did continue to correspond with her friends from the Oklahoma City survivors' group for two years afterward. She wrote to Richard Williams to say that she was moving to a new apartment in the city, had a new job, and was working with a different therapist.

I was probably the last person in the group to let go of the fantasy persona she created. Until I began working on this book, I still insisted to myself and to others that Tania's altruism was legitimate—even if her story was fabricated. I continued to believe that her heart was good and even considered that we might reestablish our friendship someday.

That all changed after I ran into her, not once, but twice last year. What are the chances of that happening in a city of eight million people?

On December 23, 2010, in the midst of the holiday rush, I was walking up West Forty-Eighth Street when, out of the corner of my eye, I spotted a familiar silhouette crossing Broadway. The woman looked like Tania. I caught up to her and noticed the familiar scent of Aromatics Elixir, Tania's fragrance. Three years had passed since I last saw her. Her hair was darker, but otherwise she hadn't changed. I reached out and placed a hand on her shoulder.

"Tania," I said softly. She jumped back, clearly startled.

"Get away from me!" she shouted. "Don't speak to me!" Her face twisted with rage and, defiantly, she thrust her middle finger at me, and then ran into the street.

I was in total shock. What had I expected? I think I thought that we would get a coffee at Starbucks, the way we used to, and talk over old times. I think I was expecting Tania, my dear friend. Concerned for her safety, I headed in the opposite direction, toward the subway. But before I descended the staircase, I looked back and saw her standing there, watching me. I realized then that I was looking at a stranger.

I punished myself for months afterward for having given up so easily. I should have persisted, I told myself. I should have followed her. I still had so many questions I wanted to ask her, and so many festering feelings about this woman I'd once thought of as one of my closest friends. I was certain I would never receive another chance to get the answers I needed to sort out my feelings. To figure out what was real and what wasn't.

I was wrong.

Nine months later, against impossible odds, I saw her again. It was Wednesday, September 14, 2011, three days after the tenth anniversary of 9/11. I was walking toward an animal shelter to adopt a kitten when Tania and her mother walked past me. She didn't notice me, but I recognized her instantly. I was shaking when I grabbed my camera out of my backpack and began to follow them down the FDR Drive. My goal was to find out where she was living now. I didn't want her to get away. I was intent on talking to Tania or Alicia or any combination. I was finishing up the documentary and wanted to give her one last chance to tell her side of the story.

I watched as they stopped along the East River to take in the sunset, and I couldn't help but notice how carefree and happy she looked. It reminded me of Tania, and I was overcome with wistful memories of our friendship. I fought the urge to run up and hug her. Then it occurred to me how much power she still had over me, and how difficult it was for me to break through the illusion of the person I wanted her to be.

I continued to follow them as they walked along the river, then up East Thirty-Fourth Street to a chic boutique hotel a block from Park Avenue. There was apparently no apartment in the city anymore. When they went inside, I sat down at a nearby bus stop, wondering what my next move should be. My mind was racing. Had she come to town for the anniversary? Had she been there somewhere at ground zero? Holding a red bandanna in tribute to Welles Crowther? Tracing David ██████ ███████'s name that was etched into the stone borders of the reflection pool onto her program, as I had done? I thought about Gerry and Linda and Janice and Brendan and Elia, and how, years later, they continued to be haunted by her betrayal.

All of the suffering Tania had caused. All of the collateral damage. Yet not a shred of contrition. Not a phone call or a letter to try to ease the burden of those she'd betrayed. How was that possible? Tania and her mother walked through the streets of New York, laughing and lighthearted like the city belonged to them. My nostalgia for what once was suddenly turned to rage.

Two hours after they ducked into their hotel, Tania emerged alone. She wore a black party dress. She looked thinner and prettier than I'd ever seen her. To my surprise, she walked to a bus stop farther down the street. Where could she be going? I wondered. Was she going as Alicia or someone else? I remembered what Sam Kedem said about the chance of her scamming someone else. "I don't know if she's doing it now," he said, "but some day she will. Absolutely."

My bottled-up rage came spilling out, and I turned on my camera and walked a long, diagonal path across the street toward where she was standing. My heart was pounding out of my chest.

She didn't recognize me at first. But as I walked closer, she spotted the camera. I saw in her eyes precisely the moment when she realized it was me. She shook her head from side to side, and her body turned rigid. I was the enemy, and she was ready for battle.

"Don't come near me, Angelo," she hissed. "Get away from me."

I didn't hold back: "How could you show up here during the tenth anniversary?" I cried. "How could you?"

Her face twisted with rage, and she lunged at me. I continued to film. She grabbed for my camera. I turned and ran, and she chased me up Lexington Avenue.

"How dare you!" I screamed. "Don't you have any feelings for the people you've hurt? Tania? Don't you have any feelings at all?" Her eyes bore into me. They were on fire. "I'm calling the police," she said, punching a number in her cell phone.

"*She's* calling the police? How ironic," I thought. I had seen enough, and I certainly wasn't going to give her the satisfaction of a confrontation with the police. I turned off the camera and walked away.

I took no pleasure in that encounter. That night, I replayed the video and cringed. I felt sad. And sorry. Did that mean I forgave her? Who the hell knows? I didn't even know who she was.

In the weeks prior to the tenth anniversary, a war of words broke out on the survivors' forum after one member questioned the veracity of another member's story. That turned into everyone doubting everyone else. Linda was so upset by the growing animosity among the members that she wrote an open letter to the group:

All: I have been reading these posts about frauds and am so depressed. STOP . . . we came here because not only as survivors but because as a nation we were wounded and devastated. We needed to find a place to come together and regroup, find friendship, and find peace. I know over the past 10 years, nothing can take all the pain away from me. All the sleepless nights wondering WHY? Trying to find a reason why I lived? THIS is why we are here. Please don't allow these posts and accusations to take away or detract from what we are here for. YES, we were devastated by Tania's actions. However, let's not give her or anyone else any more power. As we look back over the past 10 years, let's remember why we came together in the first place. We came here for EACH OTHER. I hope to see, hug, and kiss all of you next week and may God bless the souls that departed us and their families on September 11, 2001. I know none of us would ever forget why we came here in the first place. Please stay here and be part of my family.

The survivors mourned the woman who wasn't there. Their initial denial, that Tania couldn't possibly be a pretender, had eventually turned to sadness over losing their beloved friend and leader, then anger over her stunning betrayal, and, finally, acceptance and the resolve to move forward. They had come to see her as a composite of dichotomies: a gentle-hearted humanitarian on one hand, and a covetous, self-serving narcissist on the other. She was someone who could heal the deepest wounds and also inflict them. But, ultimately, the attacks on 9/11 weren't enough to destroy the survivors, and neither was she.

ACKNOWLEDGMENTS

From the Authors:

We are so grateful to have been shepherded into writing this story by our wonderful agents, David Patterson and Peter McGuigan at Foundry Media. To Jerry Kalajian of Intellectual Property Group, the talented and wonderful Martha Skolnik, and Rachel Winter for putting us all together. We are also indebted to the inspiring and talented team at Touchstone who guided us with compassion and wisdom: Matthew Benjamin, David Falk, Marcia Burch, Ashley Hewett, Meredith Vilarello, and Kiele Raymond. Finally, we would like to thank the World Trade Center Survivors' Network for their strength, courage, and generosity in sharing their journey with us.

From Robin Gaby Fisher:

To Angelo Guglielmo, you rock! Thank you for trusting me with this incredible story, and for the wonderful friendship that has grown from our collaboration. As always, to my beloved husband, Loren Fisher, for his constant love and support. To my family, Dad, Carolyn, Penny, Scott, Yvonne, Nicole, and Shawn, I couldn't love you more. To my mentors, Marilyn Dillon, Carolyn Beyrau Glickman, Fran Dauth, Jim Willse, you taught me everything about storytelling that I know. I am so grateful for my rich and enduring friendships: Jayne Daly Munoz, Amy Ellis Nutt, Mary Romano, Kitta MacPherson, Marianne Timmons, Ken Cunningham, I am humbled by your loyalty and encouragement. To Shawn Simons and Alvaro Llanos, this book thing began with you and your incredible story of courage and survival, and we ended up family. There has been no greater gift for me, and I cherish you both.

To my Rutgers' University mentor, Rob Snyder, thank you for sharing your keen intellect and for your endless patience, guidance, and support; and to my Rutgers' students, you inspire me and make me proud every single day.

Finally, to my mom, Betty Elnora Eick Milligan, whom I lost when my adult life was only just dawning, but whose wisdom has guided me to every happiness and success I have experienced since. When I think of her, I am reminded of the words of Kahlil Gibran: "The teacher who is indeed wise does not bid you to enter the house of his wisdom but rather leads you to the threshold of your mind." With more love and integrity than anyone else I have ever known, my mom gave me the courage and the will to find my way to a life with purpose and meaning. I hope she would be proud of the person I have become.

From Angelo Guglielmo, Jr.:

To my fabulous coauthor, Robin Gaby Fisher, who so generously bestowed her formidable talent, sharp wit, and insight throughout this writing. To everyone in the Guglielmo family (and Antonio), for always being there. To the wonderful author, Marian Fontana, for her compassion, love, and light in sharing her bold and courageous path with me. To Beth Dannhauser for her perception and guidance. To Alice Greenwald, Amy Weinstein, Jan Ramirez, Lynn Rasic, and the staff at the National September 11 Memorial and Museum for their warmth, insight, and recognizing "the endurance of those who survive."

To Amy Rapp and Meredith Vieira for taking a chance on me and giving a deep, vibrant life to the documentary, "The Woman Who Wasn't There." To my generous colleagues, Andy Bowley, Peter McGovern, and Alberto Chelleri, who have always believed in the film whose footage, of course, became essential research material for the book.

To Karen Seiger of Sirene MediaWorks, who always makes an adventure fun. To Chris Edwards of Production Junction for being there for me and all artists, a filmmaker's best friend forever. To Ross

Kauffman of Red Light Films for teaching me to be tougher. To Andrea Smith for her talent, red hair, and love of life.

To Lynn Tierney, Howard Cash, Rachael Grygorcewicz, and Sally Yerkovich for believing in me. To Peter Green for his expertise, artistry, and support. To Steve Dannhauser and Michael Weil of Weil, Gotshal & Manges LLP for their early advice. To Amanda Ripley for her astute perspective into the lives of survivors. To Mary Miles of Greenberg Traurig, and to the terrific director Steven Addair and producers Danielle Addair and Susann Brinkley of Shoulder Hill Entertainment. To Jaime Longhi and Jonathan Gray and Bruce Meyerson of Gray, Krauss and Des Rochers LLP. To Robert Seigel of Cowan DeBaets Abrahams & Sheppard LLP. To Steve Guglielmo. To Javier Amor of the Amor Group, Austin Murphy, David Schlamm, and Esther Muller of City Connections Realty for helping to keep me afloat during the process. To Anthony Antonello, Fred Funke, Ari Silverstein, Rob Purdy, Arsen Karougian, Matt McLaughlin, Mike Dawson, and Abe Clements for good times at the beach.

I'm also so very grateful to Jane Rosenthal of Tribeca Productions for her warmth and encouragement.

To Leah Packtor, Arlene Golonka, Joan Hazelton, and all the teachers at Francis Lewis High School who inspired me to plant seeds. To Charity James who believed in this project from the very beginning and created magic with laughter, love, and unabashed chutzpah. To Kelley McAuliffe for her fiery wisdom.

To Gabriel Amor who has been there, through the light and dark, to guide me with his expansive talent and warm heart—thanks for helping *me* off the precipice. To Kurt Griemsmann for being an amazing lifelong friend.

To my father, Angelo J. Guglielmo, Sr., for being a stellar role model and instilling in me his investigative instinct. And finally, to the magnificent writer, painter, and artist of life, Grace Guglielmo, who taught me how to make life an expedition, cultivate a garden, paint in vivid colors, and dream.